PRAISE FOR
ALL ROADS LEAD TO JERUSALEM

Jenny Jones' yearlong journey with her three children to the West Bank to bond with her husband's Palestinian family may seem like a strange place to find personal peace given the strife of the Israeli/Palestinian conflict. She takes many risks as a Muslim woman in search of answers to the difficult issues faced by the Palestinians. On return to Oregon she realizes her increased courage and self-confidence and hopes to return one day to Safa.

~REV. EDWARD HARTWELL, RETIRED EPISCOPAL PRIEST AND A FOUNDING MEMBER IF THE "INTERFAITH COMMUNITY FOR PALESTINIAN RIGHTS"

* * *

An exceptional and unique way to write about Palestine-Israel. Through her stories, Jennifer catches the attention of readers untraditionally interested in our region of the world.

~OMAR HARAMY, SABEEL ECUMENICAL LIBERATION THEOLOGY CENTER

* * *

If you want to read a book about personal hope, forgiveness, and the spirit of freedom this is the one.

A woman of integrity Jones is candid about her American privilege, small town naiveté, convictions of faith, and cultural submission. Her desire to give her children an expanded identity as Palestinian leads her to live with her in-laws for over a year in a West Bank village where new found personal freedom unfolds; she takes risks and makes decisions that are life and death as she traverses the Occupied Territories and Israel. Such risk-taking becomes a metaphor for her experience as a woman traversing religion and culture, individuality and family, belonging and freedom. She discovers there is a difference between religion and culture to the detriment of women, and thus to a whole religious community,, become merged.

Jones stirs in us the sometimes uncomfortable thoughts and perspectives born of our own beliefs and culture as we encounter the stranger in foreign lands. She challenges us to think and act beyond our need for safety and belonging especially when it compromises our integrity or dehumanizes other human beings.

For anyone who wants to get a glimpse into the tragedy of occupation here it is through the eyes of an American Muslim about one family's fight to preserve its religion, culture, role of women, protect its children, and survive. Jones portrays the effects of fear on herself and her family as they deal with the abuse, and often imprisonment of their men and young boys, by Israeli soldiers.

Jones exposes the horror and violations of Israeli occupation on the mind, body, and spirit of the Palestinian people; the acts that dehumanize another person reducing their worth and value, and erode the collective integrity of a people's way of life and culture.

Written with honesty and character Jones demonstrates, born of the evolution we witness in her, that we as finite human beings are always in motion, our daily choices no matter how messy, difficult or complex, contribute to the transformation of our lives into who we are at this moment and who we will become in the future. She discovers that belonging and freedom are fluid transcending location, culture, suffering and politics.

Through it all she finds hope for herself and her family as she discovers that her place, her belonging, isn't about one location and one set of people but about the bonds forged of the heart, forgiveness, and understanding.

~REV MONICA E. STYRON, FRIENDS OF SABEEL-NORTH AMERICA, AND
TEACHING ELDER IN THE PRESBYTERIAN CHURCH, U.S.A.

All Roads Lead To

Jerusalem

All Roads Lead To
Jerusalem

*An American Muslim Mom's
Search for Meaning in the Holy Land*

JENNIFER LYNN JONES

Library of Congress Cataloging-in-Publication Data on File

For inquiries about volume orders, please contact:

TitleTown Publishing, LLC
PO Box 12093
Green Bay, WI 54307-12093
920-737-8051

Published in the United States by TitleTown Publishing
www.titletowpublishing.com

Distributed by Midpoint Trade Books
www.midpointtrade.com

Printed in the United States of America

Interior design by Jane Perini, Thunder Mountain Design
Cover Design by Michael Short

To my children,
Ibrahim, Amani and Karim,
who learned to be brave before their time…

Contents

Introduction

At thirty-six, I lived a comfortable, Martha Stewart-inspired life in a pish-posh suburban Seattle neighborhood with my husband, Ahmad, and my three kids, Ibrahim (twelve), Amani (nine), and Karim (two). I had a family I loved, lots of (housewife) friends and a respected reputation in the local Islamic community. I tried to appreciate my life; I really did. Then one day at my nine-year-old daughter, Amani's, Taekwondo class, it all came crashing down.

Tall for her age, slim and quick-witted, Amani turned to me with a cheeky thumbs-up sign after pummeling her latest opponent—then helped him off the mat. In that instant I saw her natural confidence, self-worth and her unapologetic right to her place in the world. I couldn't help but remember that I used to feel just like her. But somewhere along the line, I lost my way and became a meek, Muslim version of my grandmother—make the dinner, put it on the table and clean it up afterward.

Once upon a time, and believe me when I say it felt like some time ago, I thought of myself as an "empowered Muslim woman" (hey, they do exist). I certainly was not the shrinking, people-pleasing shadow that many expect a "good" Muslim woman to be. No, I believed I'd actually combined a life of deep faith and personal satisfaction. In fact, I even wrote a book embraced across the Muslim world that advised other women like me on how to become one of the illusive Yetis I thought I was: a true Muslim feminist.

I received many letters from readers, some even telling me that they were inspired by my book to embark on new paths of their own. They said they had thrown off the yoke of cultural expectation, sexism and conformity that weighs on many Muslim women. I should have been pleased with that, and in some ways I suppose I was. Still, I couldn't get away from a gnawing feeling that I was, in fact, a fraud. After all, precious little of my own "great advice" had managed to stick to me.

Part One

Beginnings

CHAPTER 1

So There Was This Rabbi…

*It is the mark of an educated mind to be able to
entertain a thought without accepting it.*

- ARISTOTLE

Tall, blonde, wearing at least eight gold rings and given to tight, pencil-skirted business suits, Amy was honestly the last person I expected to convert—but there she was, standing at the microphone held by the Imam next to the grille separating us from the men. I remembered when Ahmad told me she thought I was weird for covering my hair, and that I "might as well be bald." Well, tonight she stood in my prayer gown with her blonde hair covered, just like mine.

La 'ilāha 'illallāh, Muḥammad rasūlu-llāh. "I bear witness that there is no God but Allah and Muhammad is his Messenger." She said these words in front of the whole mosque.

Takbir! shouts the Imam. "Witness!"

AllahuAkbar! "God is Great!"

Three times the men below chorus, rumbling up through the floor as if claps of thunder. Amy is a Muslim now, just like me. God help her.

Actually, it wasn't Islam that was hard. It was just hard being around those *other* Muslims. You know, the native-born kind who thought they were so much better than converts like me. And I was *not* bitter. There was no chip on my shoulder. None.

I converted to Islam quite a few years before that night in the mosque with Amy, and I held onto each of those years as a level I was holding above newbies like her. In fact, by the time she converted in the mid-nineties, I'd already been a Muslim for close to eight years and the wife of a Palestinian for four. I liked to think myself an expert in the presentation of female holiness, signified primarily by dress and a fast, obsessive study of Arab homemaking.

I also worked hard on Palestinian cooking, the Arabic language (at least enough to be able to understand what was being said about me), and even the cultural Arabic mannerisms, the lack of which, made me seem—well—a *shiksa*. After all, in our world, small nuances seemed important enough to tip the earth on its axis, and things like the proper timing of the tea service, the tone and volume of one's voice in mixed company, even the style, wrap, and color of the scarf on my head—it all seemed to have so much meaning.

Are you good enough?

Of course, my husband, Ahmad, would love to take the credit for my religion in certain circles. Islam is open to new members, and although its missionaries may lack the sophistication and savvy of other religious groups, most Muslims take tremendous pride in their growing convert pool; all the more if the convert is somehow famous, beautiful, or *white*.

It's all over the internet—lists of "famous Muslim converts" and You-Tube videos of scarf-covered co-eds who grew up Presbyterian, Baptist, or Jewish but later embraced Islam. In fact, Islam is the fastest-growing religion in the world, and its population is expected to double world-wide to 2.2 billion by the year 2030. Regardless of whether the growth is due to conversion or population increases, Muslims are extremely proud of this fact, particularly those of us who live in the West. After all, there's just something about being a quasi-hated minority that makes things like keeping score seem important—and that's where I think Ahmad's pride comes in. It's a boost to the old husbandly ego to walk into a Western mosque with a convert on his arm (well, not *literally* on the arm; men and women don't touch in the mosque).

Still, most people in our mosque know my conversion story by now, and as much as he'd like to, Ahmad can't take the credit (or the blame). That's an honor that goes to the rabbi.

Rabbi Bruce was cute for an older guy, and my freshman English teacher, Mrs. West, had an obvious crush on him. Maybe it was mutual, because she'd *somehow* managed to drag him into our backwoods Oregon farming town to give a talk on Abraham's monotheism as a supplement to James Michener's *The Source*. It was Rabbi Bruce who introduced me to Islam and, as he put it, to that religion and Judaism's "pure monotheism," a topic that was right up my alley.

I was a religious kid. That was unusual only because my family really wasn't. Like many North American families, we were nominally Christian, celebrating Easter and Christmas. However, we didn't go to church or even claim a particular denomination. Still, I remember being very serious about my bedtime prayers, obsessively requesting blessings for each family member in turn and always wrapping up by asking God to "say hi to Jesus, " of whom I'd become fond mainly through Christmas cartoon specials—*holla' to the donkey*. I assumed that I was a Christian because Christianity was the only religion I knew. It was only when I became old enough to be aware of "the Trinity," or the doctrine that defines God as three divine entities, that I began to doubt.

By all rights, I was a little young to doubt anything. At fourteen,

I was marginally into "normal" teenage things: drinking, boys, music. However, religions became my chief interest, and I even briefly joined a group then known as "the Rajneeshees." This was a controversial group whose members were best known for meditation, wearing only shades of red, having lots of sex, and taking over the small Oregon town of Antelope. As it turned out, my attraction to that group had more to do with a couple of cute twin boys my age who were adherents, rather than a real connection to Rajneesh's amorphous doctrine. So when the group was eventually driven out of the state and back to India, I was ripe to take in the Rabbi's message—and that message was a revelation.

"Islam," he said, "and Judaism are the world's only true monotheistic religions. In fact," he continued, "if you keep in mind the Trinity, Christianity could be considered a polytheistic faith."

It was the first time that I'd ever heard anyone compare Islam to Judaism and Christianity, pointing out that Islam shared many of the same Bible stories and most of the same prophets, as well as its being a monotheistic religion that might be related to the God I understood and prayed to every night. And since Rabbi Bruce went on to point out that "one doesn't really convert to Judaism without considerable difficulty," I gleaned that Islam was a pretty close alternative.

It was a surprising message—indeed, one that I suspect shocked Mrs. West and many of my religious Christian classmates, particularly my in-class nemesis, Amy "born-again" Rogers, who never missed an opportunity to point out that I "wasn't saved" and was headed to Hell. Whatever his motives, Rabbi Bruce gave me more than enough reasons to head to the library to find myself a Quran after class.

CHAPTER 2

In the Closet

All growth is a leap in the dark, a spontaneous unpremeditated
act without the benefit of experience.

- HENRY MILLER

If Ahmad liked taking the credit in Muslim circles from those who assumed I converted out of love for him, he didn't do it in general public. It isn't much fun to be a conspicuous Muslim in North America, particularly after 9-11, and it wasn't long afterward that Ahmad began to refuse to be seen with me in public when I was wearing either black scarves or *abayas*—the familiar voluminous black outer garments that many Muslim women wear, particularly in the Gulf countries. He was convinced (perhaps rightfully so), that people would think he'd forced me to wear Islamic dress.

As for me, I liked my scarf, *usually*. And I loved my comfy abayas, but that didn't mean I wasn't sometimes uncomfortable, too. Still, I had to fight a hard battle to embrace Islam alone, only a couple of months after Rabbi Bruce's visit. Given the fact that I was probably the only Muslim in the entire town, it wasn't an easy transition.

To say my typical American parents were alarmed at my choice was an understatement (odd, given that the Rajneesh crowd was well known in Oregon for taking over a small town, stockpiling Uzi submachine guns, and developing a burgeoning bio-terrorism program—and they never seemed bothered much by *them*). Still, I suppose they were comforted by the notion that my red clothes and *mala*, the beaded necklace holding a Lucite-framed picture of guru Bhagwan Shree Rajneesh, would only last as long as this latest adolescent crush. Becoming a Muslim, though, was something they couldn't understand, especially since my enchantment wasn't linked to any clear outside influence. To them, Islam was a horrible foreign choice that they supported about as much as an old-school Pentecostal family would embrace their newly outed gay son.

It wasn't long before my parents put a stop to my "nonsense," and confiscated my Quran, prayer rug (which I bought during a family trip to Disney World), and scarf, boxing them up and hiding them in the attic until I was "old enough to move out." Still, I held onto my new faith, praying—literally—in the closet or in the back yard with a beach towel on my head. Clearly, it would take a lot more than a little social discomfort for me to give up any vestige of my religion, and if it made Ahmad uncomfortable—so be it.

I was already a Muslim by the time I met Ahmad at a Future Farmers of America convention. Thrilled that it was a year that the convention would take place at Oregon State University—where they had an actual mosque—I saw it as a chance to finally meet someone "like me." Until that point, I hadn't yet met any other Muslims, and since it was well before the age of the Internet, I was forced to learn my new faith solely through the books available at our small-town library. Although it turned out that I was too shy do anything more than walk around the outside of the local mosque, when I got there I met a skinny Palestinian engineering student in the University dorms where we were staying. It turned out that, despite his rather amazing grip on 1980s-style splendor (gold necklace, flip-flops, a mustache, and playing the newest strains of Air Supply on a portable cassette recorder), he nonetheless made a significant impression on me. After all, he was the first Muslim I met, and I saw him as a shining personification of the stars on the spangled short-shorts he wore. Soon we were writing snail-mail and professing our undying love to each other. Oh, and I was all of 15 years old.

CHAPTER 3

Leaping In

*Hypocrisy is the essence of snobbery, but all snobbery is
about the problem of belonging.*

-ALEXANDER THEROUX

L ess than three years later I was free of family pressure and attending Oregon State University, my box retrieved from the attic.
Now, I was ready to cannonball into what I assumed would be
a perfect Islamic community. It would be great—all idyllic brother- and
sisterhood, pure devotion to God and prayers. I'd be able to drink from
the fount of religious knowledge and flower into Muslim maturity. And
I would belong.

I immediately began attending the local mosque, a traditional Saudi-
esque Sunni institution complete with fully separated men's and wom-
en's sections. I began to wear a headscarf and long skirts, and continued
my relationship with Ahmad, the Palestinian engineering student, but
now, it was done in person. It wasn't long, though, until members of
the mosque pointed out that having a "boyfriend" was not acceptable in
Islam, and that it would be better if I "didn't mention it to the others."

Unwilling to sin against my religion, madly in love with my *hush-
hush* boyfriend, and lacking advice on finding a middle ground—after
all, I'd only been "instructed" to hide the relationship—I immediately

turned to what seemed the only sensible choice—immediate marriage. I was nineteen, full of religious fervor, and positive that I was on the right path. I even imagined that my new husband, Ahmad, a "born Muslim," represented Islam incarnate.

I was primed to put both my husband and my marriage up on a pedestal—a perch all the more precarious for my lack of experience in the world. Therefore, I was wholly unprepared for the sometimes huge differences between Ahmad's Arabic and Palestinian culture and "ideal" Islam, where things like sexual inequality, rigid gender roles, and complex behavioral nuances were beyond my experience or understanding. The Islam of books, private faith, and reason was what had captured my heart before I'd actually met any Muslims. Muslim *culture*—influenced by national customs, conflict, prejudice, and human interest, on the other hand, only confused me, as I was unable to distinguish the difference between them.

Take, for instance, the complete separation of the sexes in the mosque, where women had their own section upstairs and were forbidden to communicate with men during community elections, debate, lectures and the like. The exception was the option to send written notes, passed down to the "brothers," who presumably would be moved to lust by the mere sound of a female voice or the fact that many mosques didn't even have a "women's section" at all, but were instead reserved wholly for men.

Even home life was a complex warren of manners and customs that I often found incomprehensible. Visiting other Muslim couples in their homes meant a complete separation between male and female guests, as well as complex and intricate hospitality rules and rituals—from the timing of the tea service to the manner of the slaughter of the meat being served. In fact, as the years went by, the sheer number of details and nuances of life in the dual-culture marriage I'd taken on was overwhelming—and almost exclusively one-sided.

In short, Arabic culture *was* Islam, and it was only after many painful lessons that I began to see that maybe there was a line separating the two—and *sometimes* the twain would meet.

Maybe it would have been fine—this difference between what I began to see as "pure" Islam and cultural Islam—*if* I could reconcile myself with the differences. Problem was, I never chose to become an Arab, or a Palestinian, and in spite of the things I admired about Arabic culture—family unity, hospitality, humor, and what seemed like a thousand other "positives"—many of which I found lacking in my own, there were also things that ate at my own sense of cultural identity which was not as easily or wisely shed as I'd supposed. I still loved things like English, American music, mixed conversation, and the assumption that women were (in theory) equal to men. Yet, in *my* Arabic-Muslim world, all of these things felt uncomfortably subversive.

Arab culture, and my naive and partially subconscious assumption that it was synonymous with Islam, was a force that wore at me, whether I understood it or not. Every time I served male guests their tiny glasses of coffee before the women (as was the "rule"), pretended to be shy and soft-spoken in Muslim company, yet outspoken in a class or with my own family, or even heard about something as extreme as honor killings or a terrorist attack on civilians somewhere in the Middle East, I felt my sense of certainty about my identity waver.

Still, I stuck it out. After all, my marriage, my three children and my place in the life I'd built meant everything to me. By my thirties, however, the opacity of my faith had all but turned to black. The pressure of life in my traditional marriage began to wear me down, but still I cooked, cleaned, had babies, managed to keep my figure, and learned when it was expected to keep my mouth shut and my eyes down. Whether it had anything to do with religion or not, I was determined to become as close to the "ideal" Muslim-American housewife as I could figure out to be. Alas, I'd sold my soul to become her. Still, I tried to ignore the loss until that day in my daughter's Taekwondo class when I realized that one day she might become just like me.

CHAPTER 4

Tranquil Unease

The ache for home lives in all of us, the safe place
where we can go as we are and not be questioned.

-Maya Angelou

I'm among the oddly populous group who somehow managed to become exactly what I hoped not to be growing up, in my case a duplicate of my stereotypical, 1950s housewife grandmother. Don't get me wrong, I loved my grandmother like crazy. Imbued with the hard, tempered stoicism of her generation and her Scandinavian upbringing, she lived the life of a perfect homemaker. Dinner was promptly at four o'clock, and was always followed with cake, made to satisfy my grandfather's sweet tooth and contribute to his sense of a smooth-running home. My sister and I would spend the odd week or two with Grandma over the spring or summer vacations, and the clockwork pace of her traditional home was a comfortable change from the latchkey, instant Ramen noodle days at my working mom's after my parents' extremely contentious divorce.

I grew up with a strong drive towards achieving the same stability, that feeling of safe, predictable normalcy that traditional homes seemed to have, and it made my quick slip into homemaker after college seem inevitable. I didn't admit it at the time—even to myself. However, I had an almost pathological need to be taken care of and made absolutely safe somehow, by a man. Of course, it was a decision based on fear, a powerful motivator. Then came the kids.

I imagine that I was like many women; I didn't find the childbearing years to be exactly fertile ground for contemplation, and the birth of each child provided just enough exhaustion to make self-reflection seem unpleasant and pointless. So, too, by the time each child reached the magical age of preschool, my accompanying relief was just enough to *mimic* an illusion of well-being and even engender a willingness to consider planning the *next* child.

Before I knew it, though, twelve years passed, and when the inertia of early motherhood finally wore off, what was left was the sudden, frightening realization that "being taken care of" was really no guarantee of safety at all. Life could change for the worst in my old-fashioned family just as easily as it could for the more progressive. It was a lesson I learned when my oldest son's liver failed one day.

This was to be a terrifying and confusing time. One day Ibrahim was a happy five-year-old, playing and going to school. The next day he was sick, yellow, on the verge of death, and literally at the top of the national organ transplant waiting list—and doctors couldn't figure out why. Although he recovered spontaneously—and rather miraculously—without the liver he was next in line for, we never found out why it happened. All I knew was that as I later watched him hug his hero, Mickey Mouse, on his Make a Wish trip to Disneyland, I was one grateful but traumatized mama. His illness removed the illusion that living cautiously was a guarantee of survival.

So by the time I reached my mid-thirties, I had a pretty home, a stable marriage, three beautiful children that I loved, and a nagging feeling that *something was wrong*—as if I'd shortchanged my future somehow. I'd never held a job, nor had I accomplished any of my high school dreams, which included writing about the Holy Land, learning Arabic, and travelling somewhere alone. *Anywhere.*

But then again, so what? It wasn't as if the world would end if I didn't work, write or travel, and as Ibrahim's health continued to improve and allowed our lives to move into a smooth pattern again, I let gratitude overtake the unease. *I should be thankful and just carry on*, I thought. As often happens in life, though, circumstances conspired to bring forth a change.

Like most Muslims living in the United States following 9-11, we faced a staggering negative backlash. We coped with a mixture of frustration, anger, and sadness, along with a general feeling that we should always be on our best behavior in public to prove that we were nothing like the monsters who flew the planes that day. Still, as the years passed, it seemed as if the feeling of *otherness* was growing instead of diminishing. And along with the rainy Northwest weather, which was itself dark, damp, and depressing, there loomed a growing feeling of alienation that began to threaten our family in unexpected ways.

Although my fear of being physically assaulted by non-Muslims diminished in the months following the 2001 attacks, the passing years saw a definite increase in a more subtle, almost psychological pressure. Like many other Muslim families in the area, we noticed more of what we called "incidents"—the insults, dirty looks, and cold-shoulders that wore down any feelings of well-being like drops of water torture. The kids and I were called "sand niggers" in the grocery store, and people would shout at us from passing cars to "go home!" (presumably to our Middle Eastern origins). Even worse, suspicious stares from our neighbors and snubs at the kids' schools, sports activities, and other gatherings took a heavy toll on us all. Just as bad, though, was how the government treated us.

Our lives now felt strange and unsettled. Suddenly, we were required to do things in the name of "security" that were once unheard of, like reporting the details of our financial transactions to our bank manager, who was somehow deputized to interrogate us about the sources and uses of our personal funds. We even received calls from the Secret Service (although I thought it was a hoax and responded with full F-bomb fury—until I realized they were actually who they claimed to be), and Ahmad was ordered to report to our local Starbucks for a "friendly chat" with an agent from the FBI. This after being turned in by a neighbor under the new "citizen vigilance program." His crime? Receiving Islamic mail in the community mailbox.

My husband had been a full citizen for at least six years, and I'd been born in the USA. However, it felt as if we were as foreign and out of place as our fellow residents saw us to be. At a time when I was becoming the least comfortable in my own skin, my outside world was now a mirror of my unease, and my older kids felt it, too. They even asked me to "please stop wearing that scarf" when I picked them up from school. The knowledge that I had, in essence, created them to suffer the same lack of belonging that plagued me made it all the harder to bear. That's when I got the bright idea. Why not try out life in Palestine—it was their father's homeland, and by extension, theirs as well. In theory a good block of time there—say, at least a year—might just be a good thing. The only catch was I'd have to do it without Ahmad, whose high-level Microsoft job required him to stay put.

I didn't want out of my life, or my marriage—not completely, anyway. But I couldn't deny that the thought of such a long span of time away from being a wife and all that it entailed—the daily major and trivial allowances, compromises, and maneuvers required in any intimate relationship—was alluring. As scary as such a long, solitary sojourn in Palestine seemed, I also knew that I might find some narrow slivers of time, opportunity and resources that I needed to make a go at a measure of a satisfying life for myself. *Yes*, I'd decided. It was a good move. Leaving my husband behind in America so I could live in the Holy Land would allow me the space I needed away from the uniquely cultural pressures of my marriage. It would also give me relief from members of my husband's local extended family, which consisted of a singularly high-maintenance motley crew of cousins, nieces, and brothers—all successfully immigrated to the United States, married and blessed with kids of their own.

It wasn't that I didn't care about them all, especially the kids, but my rabid desire for what I then understood to be a "perfect," stable family life also compelled me to be the whole gaggle's social manager. That meant arranging birthdays, Thanksgivings, Islamic holiday dinners, babysitting, play dates—as many and as perfectly designed as I could. It was exhausting, especially because it was all very one-sided (a fact that somehow failed to dawn on me). I was the easy one, the welcoming one, the family "yes girl."

Sure, it was my own damn fault. I certainly wasn't doing it all out of the goodness of my heart. I believed that by so doing, I'd be cementing my place in the family, in spite of my "otherness." Add to that a meager sense of boundaries, and I became a fantastic, beautifully designed doormat. In fact, at one point, I even allowed my husband's cousins and brothers to move into our home (at the time, a one-bedroom apartment), necessitating that I wear my scarf (required in their presence) twenty-four hours a day.

And then there was the fact that I'd never lived on my own. Sure, I loved my husband, but there is something to be said for waking up in the morning and deciding what you want to do with your day without discussing it with anyone, or even imagining what their preferences might be. I suppose that for many who have lived alone, this is a dubious benefit, but for me it was a completely novel experience that held great appeal; here was a large span of time in which I could make all of the decisions, tiny or large, without taking another adult's opinion or preferences into account. Of course, I would still have to please the kids, but I was the mom calling the shots. It was a whole different ball game.

Most important of all, though, was the fact that my kids were growing older, and I desperately wanted them to somehow belong in a way that was eluding me, in spite of my best (if misguided) efforts. I knew that I wanted them to be as comfortable with their Palestinian identities as they would someday be with their American ones. This would give them the option to live in either of the cultures when it came time to start lives of their own. Perhaps they could even combine them somehow. I knew that they deserved to know both worlds, and I reasoned that living a year or so in Palestine would probably be long enough for the kids to bond with their family, learn the language, and figure out the culture.

Yes, it was a good plan, I convinced myself, and during the months leading up to our departure, it became my mantra.

It was a typically cool May morning in Seattle, and Ahmad took his time loading our giant suitcases into the minivan. Although he told me that he was excited and grateful that I was willing to take the kids to bond with his mom and dad and the rest of the clan in the family village, I knew that Ahmad was nervous about my ability to stick it out and learn to take care of the kids in a complicated and sometimes dangerous place.

But the hardest thing for him to face was the fact that he would soon be spending a huge chunk of time alone, able to see his wife and kids only through a choppy Skype connection. As for me, I was still crying in our upstairs bathroom—trying to recover from the panic attack I just *knew* my mother had wished on me the moment I'd told her about my plan to haul her beloved grandkids to the Occupied West Bank. In spite of months of relative confidence, that morning saw me convinced that I was about to make a horrible mistake.

Glaring at myself in the mirror, I cursed my eyes and their tendency to swell like a boxer's after anything more than two consecutive tears. *It's normal to be nervous*, I tried to convince myself, finally chewing up a Valium while I held a cold, wet washcloth against my puffy eyelids. Problem was, I knew that the chances of me sticking it out for an entire year in the West Bank, let alone Safa, the tiny village where my husband grew up, were slim.

There was no denying it…even Ahmad, who had no choice but to stay at home and work anyway—you don't just give up and leave a good job behind for a year, especially in a bad economy, seemed to readily join the betting pool against me, even making the occasional snide remark about my slim-to-none chances of holding down a job, taking care of the kids on my own, and traipsing around one of the most dangerous regions on the planet.

Only days before, I'd been able to confidently argue with my mother in favor of my plan, yet right then, with only a couple of hours left before our flight, my mind seized on the realization that she and Ahmad were probably right on the mark. I didn't speak the language well, barely knew his family, and tended to be anxious; an affliction hardly likely to subside in a *war zone*. Add to these the fact that I'd never done anything on my own during our short visits there with Ahmad alongside—where I'd only managed to distinguish myself as a shy, clinging, wide-eyed coward who never even went out to buy a Pepsi on her own—and you could see why I was truly the sucker bet.

For some inexplicable reason, though, I was still determined to go. I had a white-knuckle grip on this trip as *the* opportunity, my quick grab into the current of opportunities that seem to speed by at the bend of mid-life. On one hand, I knew that it didn't make sense to most people.

After all, we weren't exactly hopping a plane for Hawaii. Still, I reasoned, Jewish mothers seeking to immigrate to Israel did not usually encounter the gasps and looks of horror that my news evoked in others. They just made me all the more determined that my kids, as half-Palestinians, deserved the same right to visit or live in their homeland as their Jewish cousins.

Indeed, by the time I was done applying my heavy-handed reasoning to the issue of going to Palestine, I'd managed to almost convince myself and my husband that it would be crazy *not* to go. Things were going south for Muslims here in the United States, and my kids deserved to experience their Palestinian heritage, develop a relationship with their grandparents, and master their father's native language, especially before adolescence permanently snuffed out the appeal of things like donkey rides, bleating sheep, and scores of fun-loving cousins. It was as George Eliot wrote, "We could never have loved the earth so well if we had no childhood in it."

And they wouldn't be kids forever.

It sounded reasonable.

It *did*.

CHAPTER 5

Gold, White Satin, and Scent of Skunk

Never forget what you are, for surely the world will not.
Make it your strength. Then it can never be your weakness.
Armor yourself in it, and it will never be used to hurt you.

- GEORGE R.R. MARTIN, *A GAME OF THRONES*

Ahmad had reason to be skeptical about my decision to go to Safa, but I could see that he was also hopeful and maybe even a little excited that the kids could have a chance to get to know Palestine and his family. It was a pretty sweet deal, actually. He could still keep the high-powered job he loved, and I could handle all of that pesky teaching-the-kids-about-being-Palestinian stuff. It was kind of a crazy arrangement, but then again, we hadn't really thought through the logistics of raising kids in two cultures.

Unlike all the other Muslim families that we knew in our Seattle suburb, we were the only mixed marriage around, and that meant that my kids were also the only ones who really couldn't speak Arabic. After all, their father spent long hours at work, so they couldn't really learn the language from him, and although I could understand quite a bit and even communicate in a basic way, there was no way I wanted them to start imitating my Arabic (which lacked one simple, yet important thing—conjugated verbs). And then there was the fact that my oldest son, Ibrahim, didn't start speaking at all until he was nearly four years old—yet another anxiety-producing quirk. And then, there was his un-explained liver failure, which would have driven me to drink had alcohol been permitted in Islam (thank God it wasn't). Let's just say that after more than eight years of intense speech therapy, I wasn't messing around with bilingual experimentation until he was well on the road to solid communication.

Unfortunately, language wasn't the only difference between my kids and their peers. Although I hadn't anticipated it, and for years worked hard against it, the gulf between my kids and those from non-mixed households seemed to grow with their ages. It was hard for them to make friends both inside the Muslim-American community and the larg-er mainstream American one, and I partly blamed myself.

The Arab-Muslim community in our area of Washington State was a very small world, and it was through the various women's gatherings that children stayed in touch with each other and developed friendships. Un-fortunately, the community was also very insulated, and it was extremely uncommon for any of the women that I knew to have friendships with non-Arabs. Although I tried hard for many years to integrate and partici-pate in the community, it was rare for us to be included, and that affected the kids and their friendships.

Once, frustrated by the problem, my husband asked a Palestinian friend's husband why we weren't often remembered for their get-togethers. His response, "It's just easier because they don't want to speak English."

It hurt to think that I was my kids' liability.

It was the same with the non-Muslim Moms I knew from my chil-dren's public schools, even before 9-11. It wasn't as if the women were unfriendly or bigoted. I suppose it was just that we were so different, especially because of my dress (which usually came up early in conver-sations). I don't think it was intentional. It was just easier for us to be overlooked for play dates.

And then, there was the fact that I had definite issues. Already prone to social anxiety, it was hard for me to always put out the seemingly constant extra effort to explain myself to new people, or to always be the one to take the initiative in relationships. I was always the "other" in both worlds, and it was exhausting. In Palestine, I hoped, the kids would be surrounded by family, cousins, and peers, so I would be less of a factor because the entire village was essentially family, in one way or another. And best of all, we would no longer be a religious minority. It would be the first time my kids would know what it was like to be "like everyone else."

Ahmad and I were married for almost three years before our first trip to his native village. We had wed in a tiny private Islamic ceremony in our squalid university apartment in Oregon. It was 1992, and the local Mosque refused to allow us to marry there, citing vague "problems with Muslims marrying foreigners" (probably referring to the disastrous crash-and-burn "green card marriages" that are common among young Arab students seeking coveted American citizenship). Not to be stymied, however, we managed to get the job done on our own by gathering three of my husband's friends to write out and witness the simple contract that is the basis of all Islamic marriages.

The wedding itself was surprisingly easy. In fact, there were no vows at all. Instead, as in all Islamic marriages, the union was based on a contract between the bride (if she has been married before), and the groom. If the bride is previously unmarried, however, the rules stipulate that she must have a guardian (usually her father). In my case, because I had no Muslim family, I needed to appoint an upstanding man to represent me as my guardian, or *wali*. And I chose an Iranian man named Ali, a friend's husband, to step into the role.

So that was all we needed, aside from a written contract stating our intention to be married and my "guardian's" permission. There was no wedding dress, but we invited three guests and I sported a sixty-dollar wedding band after the ceremony. Oh, and a two-dollar dowry that my new husband had to borrow from a friend.

All in all, it was a pretty austere affair, and I kept it secret from my family, afraid to upset them even more after they'd discovered that I'd been wearing Islamic-style dress, "like a freak," on campus. Of course, I could have just waited a few more years to get married, but I was nineteen and feeling more than ready to start my "grown-up life."

As for Ahmad, he was a bit braver and only waited a year to tell his family about our marriage. Still, they weren't happy at the news, and his mother reportedly spent a week in her room crying over the loss of her son to an "Amerikeeya." Knowing this didn't help my confidence as we emerged from a taxi to face the village throng for the very first time. Thankfully, I'd managed to learn enough polite, parroted phrases and behaviors to merit a warm welcome and a demand—three days later—that we have a "proper" Palestinian wedding.

Our Palestinian wedding was many things, but it wasn't lonely. Imagine three days of belly dancing parties and a day perched atop a platform in a white, marshmallow gown, cemented hair, hooker-inspired makeup, and layers of solid gold jewelry that would put a 1980s rapper to shame. It was an awesome kitsch-fest, and might have been a pretty good memory if not for the disaster in the beauty salon that day.

Palestinian brides traditionally go with close female relatives to a salon to be styled for the party, a favorite activity for village women, as it's the only chance they have to dress up and be sexy under their black *abayas*. Afterward, they stride into the segregated party, ready to unveil and shine, each hoping to be judged by the other women in attendance as the most beautiful of all.

At the time, I didn't really understand all the fuss about looking beautiful for a bunch of other women, but I went along with it. My Bethlehem beautician produced her vision for me and my sister-in-laws, who came out looking like exotic desert beauties. I, of course, was a different story.

Layers of kabuki-white foundation, thick black eyeliner, and Christmas-red lipstick turned her vision of me into a bad hallucination, especially on my already pale, green-eyed features. Even worse was my hair, styled by a short woman with a Friar Tuck bald spot and thick glasses that magnified her eyes into giant black orbs. Somehow, she'd managed to coax my bangs into a perfectly formed, rigid wave, dusted at the crest with iridescent glitter ready to break on the smooth beach of my forehead. The true glory, though, was the pair of tightly coiled blond ringlets that boinged straight out from the sides of my ears like Slinkys. It was horrible.

I didn't want to be fussy, but I just couldn't stand it, so I gingerly dipped into my shallow vocabulary pool and threw out a half-formed sentence that was received like fish to a school of sharks.

"Please…um…makeup not pretty to my eyes…"

At this, Miss Peepers smiled, the corners of her lips upturned in derision, and sneered, *Khalis ya binit!*, "Enough girl!" She quickly pushed the jar of cold cream I was reaching for out of my grasp, and then her coworker chimed in.

Yimkin Binit…she laughed, "Maybe a girl," which meant, "She?! A virgin? Yeah, Right!"

In American terms, she'd called me a slut—one of the worst insults in the Arab world. And nobody in the room, not even my sister-in-laws, said a word to defend me. It was then that I realized that my prestige level was at rock-bottom. After all, a skunk called "stinky" certainly would never take offence. So, why would a Western woman be insulted by a comment insinuating that she was somehow "loose?" It was simply a given.

This was a traumatic moment that left me with a bitter taste that lasted for many years, a moment that shook my confidence that I'd ever really fit into this new society, and a moment I subconsciously vowed never to repeat—whatever the cost!

CHAPTER 6

The Culture of Marriage

*I think women dwell quite a bit on the duress under which they
work, on how hard it is just to do it at all. We are traditionally
rather proud of ourselves for having slipped creative work in
there between the domestic chores and obligations. I'm not
sure we deserve such big A-pluses for all that.*

-Toni Morrison

The time my new husband and I spent in Palestine only amounted to a few weeks, but I spent the following years desperately
trying to be the good Arab homemaker I imagined I should be.
Rather than a healthy desire, however, it became pathological, ultimately
malignant. There is a saying that "housework, done right, can be deadly."
I think it was supposed to be a joke.

Oh sure, I knew that I probably had some lingering childhood trauma left over from my parents' divorce, some need to pick what I saw as
a super-traditional and comfortably rigid family model to mold myself
into, like a baby soothed by excessive swaddling. Add to that the kind of
humiliation I'd felt in the wedding salon, and I believed I had to prove
that I could be "as Arab as the Arabs."

I worked on my Arabic and mastered as many of the cultural nuances that I could—enough to impress the growing throng of my hus-

band's relatives who were relocating from Palestine to Seattle as part of the high-tech boom. I cooked, dressed, and behaved as Palestinian as an American girl from Oregon could, and even began doing things I didn't agree with, and weren't "Islamic" at all, but were cultural expectations. These included serving men before women, giving men the best portions of the food, staying out of sight when men visited, always keeping my voice low and my manner demure, and never laughing out loud. They were all things that bought me acceptance, but nonetheless ate at my soul because I didn't believe in them.

It has been said that "in order for something to keep its best nature, it must be put to its best use." Mindlessly emulating a culture that I didn't truly embrace on principle wasn't my best use, and believe me, my nature suffered. I became depressed but kept up the pretense of acceptance. After all, I still wanted to get as far away from that "skunk syndrome" as possible.

My solution was distraction. I had babies and I worked even harder. By the time my daughter was a busy toddler, my oldest son, Ibrahim wasn't talking and then got sick; dealing with my depression became a luxury I couldn't afford. I turned to antidepressants for as much relief as they could give me. Still, the years saw my depression linger, slowly transforming under the surface, and sharpening into a bitterness that was becoming impossible to for me to ignore.

Trying to be the "perfect wife" no longer did it for me. I didn't want to serve men before women, and what did that mean, anyway? And I wanted to laugh as often and as loud as I felt the need to do so. I, and the forces of life-experience and maturity, had merged to create a recognition of the difference between faith and culture, the limits of belonging, and the importance of personal integrity. I began to long for the freedom to develop the authenticity I'd never given myself before marriage.

Part Two

Destination: The Holy Land

CHAPTER 7

Home in Safa

Beginnings are always messy.

-JOHN GALSWORTHY

It took fifteen hours to fly from Seattle to Amman, Jordan, followed by a full day of lines, inspections, and interrogation at the scorching hot Israeli border. This multi-day journey to the West Bank is ordinarily a tough trip for adults, but throw in a toddler and two tired kids and it becomes a living hell, especially when Karim, my two-year-old, threw up in the middle of a metal detector before we cleared Israeli customs.

Finally, after passing our last inspection, we jumped into a taxi for the drive through the white-hot hills of the Judean desert to the village. It was only May, but the temperature was hovering around 115 degrees, and when I touched my son I could tell he still had a fever. The car had no air conditioning, so I held Karim next to the open window until we passed the main checkpoint, where an Israeli soldier slung his rifle to admire our Disney passport covers. Finally, we had arrived in the Holy Land!

When we arrived in Safa, my husband's family crowded around the taxi. There were aunts and uncles, cousins, brothers and sisters…as usual, too many to count, greeting us in typical Palestinian fashion, with hugs and kisses all around, followed by a traditional welcome meal. My seventy-five-year-old mother-in-law and three of my sisters-in-law: Asya, Sawsan, and Sa'eda, prepared us *Mansaf*, a dish of lamb cooked in yogurt served over a table-sized platter of steaming rice and sprinkled over with fried pine nuts, minced, bright-green parsley and sliced lemons.

I appreciated their collaboration because they hadn't really gotten along since my brother-in-law, Khalid (Asya's husband), married Sawsan a couple of years earlier after his brother died in a car crash. We were exhausted and jet-lagged, and although Karim was no longer vomiting, he was burning up with fever. Still, we followed custom and finished the meal, along with the obligatory rounds of tea and Nescafé, before I finally stood to take the kids "home." First, though, I asked another of my husband's brothers, Dr. Muhammad, a general practitioner, to take a look at Karim, who was getting worse.

We crossed the dirt road to our new house. It was an empty, hulking stone building still under construction, and we tried to settle in, but Karim, who had seemed to get better after a night's sleep, became ill again. In fact, he was getting so dehydrated that Dr. Muhammad suggested I take him to a children's hospital, the best one in the area—run by a Catholic charity in Bethlehem.

Although this wasn't my first visit to the West Bank, I'd never spent more than three weeks at a time there, and thankfully, I hadn't needed a hospital before. Unfortunately, my first dose of Palestinian health care didn't go well. I expected it to be poor—and it was, but that wasn't the problem. What surprised me the most during the long night I spent sitting next to Karim's metal hospital crib was how mean the nurses were. I watched them sleep through alarms at their desks, not bothering to wash their hands between patients, yelling at the mothers, and allowing German tourists (presumably donors) to photograph the sick children through the large sliding-glass doors on the ward.

I was jet-lagged, worried sick and pissed-off, which was probably what caused me to finally stage a mini-revolt with the other mothers on the ward. That culminated in a full-blown screaming match until the head nun finally intervened.

Thankfully, Karim rallied enough to go home, but I left shaken and more apprehensive than ever: afraid that I'd placed my kids at risks I hadn't anticipated. Moreover, the experience brought back feelings of worry and impotence that I had struggled with during Ibrahim's brush with death, concerns that I'd thought were long forgotten. I decided that even if I was being paranoid, I would be sure to buy an Israeli-licensed car so if I ever needed to drive one of my children to a hospital again, we could go to a modern one in Jerusalem.

I'd quickly learned that if you were out on the roads in the West Bank, you'd see a difference between the license plates. Like a passport, the colors designated where the cars (not just the people) were allowed to go. By and large, it meant that anyone with a yellow plate (Israeli citizens and foreigners) could drive from the Red Sea on the south to the Lebanese border at the northernmost tip (provided they stayed out of Palestinian only villages and towns). Palestinians from the West Bank, however, were restricted to driving so called "Arab cars," with green or blue licenses so they could easily be spotted as such. They were restricted to designated roads within the West Bank only. These cars were never allowed to cross into any part of Israel over the Green Line, including Jerusalem. It was a huge difference, and as a tourist living in the West Bank, I was fortunate to be able to choose between the two.

My husband and kids held Palestinian passports, in addition to their US ones. However, because of strict Israeli immigration laws (that also apply in the West Bank because Israel controls all of the Holy Land's borders), I could not qualify for one. That meant that every time I came back to this country, I would have to apply for a visa of up to three months.

While having to renew the visa was going to be hassle, it was worth it just to have the car alone.

Of course I felt guilty for using a privilege that so many Palestinians didn't have. Still, solidarity only goes so far when you have kids involved, so you take whatever protections you can. A yellow plate meant freedom to go wherever I needed to if the shit hit the fan, and I'd take what I could get in such a situation. However, there were strings attached to that choice, like being mistaken for an Israeli settler in the West Bank and having someone put a rock—or a Molotov cocktail—through our windshield.

Still, I decided that the benefits outweighed the risks, especially if I ever needed to get the kids to a modern hospital. Ultimately, I bought a tiny, used VW Polo from an Palestinian dealer in East Jerusalem and hoped for the best.

CHAPTER 8

The Princess in her Castle

Above all, you must fight conceit, envy,
and every kind of ill-feeling in your heart.

-ABRAHAM CAHAN

W e began to settle into our house, locally dubbed "the castle,"
by the villagers because of its hulking size and its ornate exterior—pillars, arches, and balconies, surrounded by a little
peach orchard and stacked stone fences. It really was quite beautiful, and
I loved to stand on the roof where I could see the entire village laid out
in a vista of vineyards, sky, and low, rolling hills. Inside, though...well, it
needed some work. Actually, lots of work.

The house was virtually empty when we arrived, so I bought some
furniture and a television to make it homier. Still, it was only habitable
on the first floor, lacked reliable electricity, had no heat and was bordered
by Safa's communal tombs (a negative best understood on a misty, wolf-
howling night).

The biggest problem, though, was the half-finished main stairwell,
with its four stories open to the sky. Because it was the end of May, the
hole in the roof wasn't such a big deal—except for the swarms of mosquitoes, wayward bats, and a rockingly loud muezzin call from the next-

door mosque. However, in a few months, winter's wind and rain would make that opening more of a problem.

It was obvious that I needed to hire construction workers to close the stairwell and connect the house to electricity, but I also knew this was going to be a major inconvenience. Safa was still one of the most conservative villages in the area, and that meant that unrelated men and women typically didn't talk to each other unless they really, *really*, had to. Because we had only arrived a couple of weeks ago, I would have to ask a male family member to supervise (and chaperone) the work being done. I was already becoming overwhelmed with what seemed like almost constant visits from my mother- and sister-in-laws, cousins, aunts and nieces. They all seemed hell-bent on helping me learn proper Palestinian housekeeping. They even went so far as to climb through my barred windows if I didn't open the door quickly enough when they knocked on the door (which they only did if they found it locked). What felt like their constant inspections and critiques—all in Arabic—were starting to get to me and my North American sense of space and privacy. Still, the house needed the work just to make it livable, so I finally asked my father-in-law to hire a contractor.

The first project on the list was to install radiators for the coming winter, which I'd been told were surprisingly cold. Khalid, my brother-in-law, hired three local men to do the work. Although it meant that even more of our privacy was gone (now, with men in the house, I had to wear my scarf inside as well as out), I knew it would be worth it. After all, even in the heat of early summer, I could imagine how cold the stone, high-ceilinged rooms must become in winter. Plus, I had a million things to do, including finding an Arabic tutor for the kids. It would certainly be easier to be out of the house when the men were around.

But then, my mother-in-law told me in slow, simplified Arabic, that it was *Ayb*, or "shameful," if I failed to provide home-cooked lunches to the workers each and every day. This was especially bad news because, based on the existing state of the house, the workers would probably be around for an entire year!

I was terrified of displeasing my mother-in-law, especially so early on. At seventy-five, despite her petite size and frail health, she was one of *the* forces to be reckoned with in the village. She'd even had her arm broken in a rock-throwing fight with her neighbors a couple of years earlier.

That's not to say that she lacked a sense of humor—it was rather impish, and came out in wicked little bursts here and there. But she was still, first and foremost, the matriarch of the family. Still, I had to tell her about a job I'd arranged for myself while still in America. I'd been hired to tutor English part time in Hebron—which I was supposed to start in a month's time. However, there was no way I could do that, take care of the kids alone, and cook huge noontime meals every day.

Unfortunately, it seemed that I was right to be nervous, after all. By the time my mother-in-law's sugar-cube had dissolved in her tea, she'd told me to forget the whole idea of work. After all, she reasoned, I would be too busy. As she already knew, my plan was to home school the kids so that they wouldn't fall behind with their schoolwork back home, and I had to run the house, cook for the men…ergo, there wouldn't be enough time for "silly" things outside the village. If it wasn't clear to me before, it was then: I needed to think of a way to keep my job, and fast. After all, it was the first job I'd had in years and I really wanted to keep it—not to mention that it was my only excuse to get out of the village.

CHAPTER 9

Woman's Work

Not only is women's work never done,
the definition keeps changing.

-BILL COPELAND

lthough it had only been a few weeks since our arrival, I could tell that my mother-in-law didn't like me very much. Whereas before, my visits with her were always short and buffered by my husband's presence or the limitations of my meager Arabic, now things were drastically different. It wasn't only because I was alone, but also because I could increasingly actually decipher some of the language—and one of the first things that became crystal clear was that she still wished her son had married an Arab Palestinian instead of me.

Of course, this wasn't exactly a revelation. Even my parents were less than pleased when I married Ahmad instead of a good-old, all-terrain-vehicle-riding, duck-hunting native Oregonian. Her attitude still hurt my feelings, though, and my skin prickled whenever I heard the word, *ajnabeeyah*, "foreign woman."

It didn't take long before word filtered back to me through the village grapevine that she thought I was a spoiled, wasteful woman, and that one of her goals was to teach me to be a better wife. And although I tried to keep a detached sense of humor about it—after all, she was a

75-year-old illiterate Bedouin woman who'd spent her years living in tents, raising sheep for a living, and giving birth 15 times at home—I couldn't deny that it hurt. Still, I couldn't exactly force her to like me, so I decided that the only solution was to ignore the problem and try not to provoke her too much. Maybe eventually I'd grow on her.

In the meantime, I came up with a bright idea: I'd ask my sister-in-laws, Asya and Sa'eda, if they would be willing to cook extra food on the days I was out at work. They cooked everyday anyway, I reasoned, and lived right across the road from me. In exchange, I could buy both families' supplies (no small thing, considering they had twelve kids between them). To my delight, they readily agreed when I asked if they would be interested in helping out. Only things didn't exactly work out as I anticipated.

Unfortunately, my first day at work was also the same day that I found out my mother-in-law was snooping through my garbage to see the amount and kinds of foods I'd been buying from the store. Over here, cola and fresh milk were considered luxuries, and I supposed that she thought she'd caught me red-handed in wretched excess because I always had them on hand. More, I found a trail of water from my clothes line to her house from her swiping laundry off my line before dawn—presumably because she found my scrubbing skills less than satisfactory. Add to that the rumor filtering back across the street that my sisters-in-law were calling me a princess behind my back.

Perfect.

Had just one of these events come to my attention on that particular day, I might have been able to control my temper, but the quick succession of what felt like an onslaught of negative judgment frayed my last nerve. As fast as a snowflake in Hades, I lost it, and I let my initial impression of detached, benevolent understanding—one I'd been trying so hard to present—boil over in flames. I threw on a scarf and speed-walked across the road to Asya's house, where I burst into her kitchen, grabbed a couple of the fresh chickens, heads a-loll, and announced in my best Arabic, "I am *not* a princess!" before I stomped home like a pissed off–well—princess. Thankfully, I finally discovered a solution to the lunch problem—and for the evil sisters-in-law. Unfortunately, this would take some time.

Of all the family members in Safa (and the whole village was related to each other in some way), my favorite was Ahmad's older sister, Huda, and her family. Always kind, welcoming and humble, Huda was also funny as hell, and she didn't seem to look at me with the same reserve as most of the other women in the family did. It also didn't hurt that she didn't like Sa'eda and Asya much, either.

It was Huda who came up with plan B—for me to prepare the construction men's food late at night and have her teenaged daughters, Manar and Rawan, warm and deliver the food at the appropriate time to their uncle—who happened to be one of the workers. In one fell swoop, it solved the lunch problem, which had started to feel ridiculously insurmountable. Of course, I knew that my mother-in-law probably wouldn't like it, but I tried to appease her as much as I could without quitting my job—especially because I hadn't even started yet!

CHAPTER 10

Angels in the Holy Land

I do not want to be the angel of any home: I want for myself what I want for other women, absolute equality. After that is secured, then men and women can take turns being angels.

-AGNES MACPHAIL

My first day on the job teaching went well. I'd been hired by the husband of a friend, who was kind enough to offer me an obscene amount of money in Palestinian terms to teach his prize engineers advanced English at his small startup in Hebron, and I was excited to meet my first students—whom I intentionally messed with in an introductory email, threatening "wrath" on any slackers among them.

It was a beautiful, sunny Monday afternoon, and the short, twenty-minute drive through the vineyard-covered hills was uneventful except for the single checkpoint I had to cross between towns, which turned out to be a quick and simple passport check. After some difficulty facing the peerlessly aggressive Hebron drivers, the city's roundabouts, and finally figuring out that in the Holy Land a yellow stoplight literally means get ready to go rather than ready to stop, I found the right building and rode the elevator up to the company's offices.

When I entered the office everyone seemed confused by me—which I later learned was because their boss had failed to mention that I was a Muslim (and with a name like Jenny Jones, who could blame them)? But they did seem excited and willing to work hard, especially when I told them I believed in novels, stand-up-comedy, and movies as key resources—and that I was (mostly) kidding about my wrath.

Thankfully, they were friendly and seemed eager to learn, if slightly intimidated by my rapid-fire English (which I expected them to try and keep up with from the start). They were also all from the "city," and I could see by their bug-eyed reactions when I told them that I lived in Safa that they might be able to give me a sense of fresh perspective when the time came.

After the two-hour class, I hurried home as fast as my little car would take me; eager to show my in-laws that my job wasn't such a big deal after all, and since Grandma was watching the kids (because, according to her, it wasn't fair for her son to pay his hard-earned money for a baby-sitter), she would be the first to see that it would all work out just fine.

When I got home, though, I found my house in an uproar. Not only was Grandma missing in action but so were my older kids—who were already reveling in their newfound freedom to roam the village, and were probably off playing with their cousins somewhere—leaving only my two-year-old, alone in the care of his seven-year-old cousin, Jamal, whom I found lying bruised and crying on the couch after losing a game of death-wish limbo with our industrial-strength steel garage door.

A few minutes later, my mother-in-law returned to the scene from wherever she'd been, yelled at Jamal, and, after making sure he could walk normally, sent him home with the threat of a beating. She then turned to me with a disapproving look. *See what happens when you're away?*

I did…and more clearly than she could have imagined, but because custom dictated an almost complete deference to one's parents (and in-laws), I bit my tongue, said nothing, thanked her for her babysitting, and wished her a good evening—all while wondering silently what the hell I was going to do.

That night, I was washing the day's dishes, scrubbing absent-mindedly, still thinking about the problem and wondering if I should just quit the stupid job, when my thoughts were suddenly interrupted by a shriek behind me. Spinning around, I turned to see Amani staring up at the cursed stairs where Karim had climbed up to the first flight, and was making for the second—right next to the edge of the open stairwell. Dropping the soapy plate from my hands, I ran towards him and sprinted up the steps, just in time to catch him by his ankle as he slipped over the side. For a horrifying moment, he was swinging above the cement floor, two levels below.

I felt sick—just sick—he could have died, and for what? Because I was so wrapped up in my agenda; the job, my problems with the other women, that I left such a glaring problem as an open pit of death in the middle of my house for my kid to fall into?

I carried Karim to bed, a million miserable thoughts swirling in my mind. Once he was settled, I headed to the bathroom, sat on the edge of the tub, and cried.

My mother-in-law was right. I should have stayed home where I belonged, I told myself again and again.

It was becoming painfully obvious that the Holy Land probably wasn't the best place to try for a radical self-transformation, at least, not for me. After all, if I'd wanted to become more of an authentic person, less burdened by the pressure to act the perfect Muslim woman/wife/mother and instead become the woman I needed to be, well, going for it in the Holy Land was probably a mistake. After all, one could argue that the whole problem of women not feeling good enough about themselves had originated on this very soil.

From the earliest recorded civilizations in the region, women have been measured by the extent of their self-sacrifice—a tradition introduced in holy books and raised to an extreme by cultural forces. Today in the Holy Land, the tradition continues through the stealthy use of flattery. The pious woman works her fingers to the bone, a Jewish woman has a "price above rubies," a faithful "silent and loving" Christian woman is a "gift of the Lord," and the religious Muslim wife and mother finds that "heaven lies under her feet." All these women know the seductive charm that spiritual accolades hold for the sad, tired, and uncertain heart. Still, many forget that there's something called "interpretation," that male scholars of each faith have accorded to women that leaves them with the short end of the stick.

It could be said that even the Western ideal of "the angel in the house" came from the history of this land, an angel the great Virginia Woolf described as, "intensely sympathetic, charming, and utterly unselfish," as well as one who "...excelled in the difficult arts of family life, and sacrificed daily." This "angel," according to Woolf, always puts others first, "If there was a chicken, she took the leg; if there was a draught she sat in it."

Sure, Palestinian culture is still rooted here in the Holy Land, and they breed their angels by old-school ideals, but what of the West? My Swedish grandmother was possessed by something that told her to always "take the leg," and she was a Christian woman—but from where do Judeo-Christian mores actually spring?

Yes, I decided...the angel was born here in this rocky soil, and I would follow in Virginia's bloody footsteps—only I was going to kill *my* angel in her lair.

"If only I was home where I belong."

That angel was a cold-hearted bitch. She deserved to die.

To be honest, I *had* tried to kill off my angel back in America, but it was a half-hearted attempt. I'd been writing my first book and had run into the resistance that always seemed to pop up like a prop in a funhouse when I tried to work on anything "extra" that took time away from the family. Then, as now, I suffered from the double-whammy of my own cultural beliefs about what made a "good woman," as well as my husband's inherited expectations. I cooked, cleaned, kept the house in repair, cared for the kids, drove my son to his speech therapy four days a week (a three-hour commute), cooked some more, home-schooled, and then applied a fresh layer of lipstick as my husband's key turned in the door. The only writing I could do was bits and pieces scribbled in "stolen" moments.

It was as the poet, Adrienne Rich, so perfectly expressed it; I wrote my book while "waiting for the iron to heat." It was a frustrating process, painful, exhausting, and even disappointing. But in Safa, despite its rigid social structure, I had a rare opportunity—I was temporarily un-pinned from the daily pressures of marriage, and that was no small thing.

Yes, I sat on that bathtub crying after my first day of work, not only out of fear for my son (although that was a major part), but also for the years of guilt and pressure that had held me back from experiencing life for so long. I cried out of frustration at the constant barter and trade I'd run (and I believe many married women run) in exchange for too few moments of freedom. I didn't come here to stay the same, or even more likely, more of a model of sacrifice. Of course, there had to be a reasonable balance.

CHAPTER 11

Solomon's Playground

Keep me away from the wisdom which does not cry,
the philosophy which does not laugh and the greatness
which does not bow before children.

-KHALIL GIBRAN

The morning after Karim's close call on the stairwell, I woke up early. I now realized that I was out of my frickin' mind for leaving the house in such a dangerous state, something I could partly blame on a delusional case of "travelers omnipotence"—that strange feeling of invincibility that sometimes crops up in a new locale, as if the rules of common sense at play back home in the *real* world somehow no longer apply. Although there was nothing like a West Bank version of *Girls Gone Wild!* to lure me into temptation, my having considered it okay to leave a four-story hole in the middle of my house had to be just as mind-bendingly stupid. It only took that one moment the night before, though, to snap my common sense back on board with a vengeance. Now, all thrusters were on fire, full speed ahead, with visions of Karim dead at the bottom of the stairwell.

I crawled out of bed and padded across the cool stone floor, careful not to wake the kids splayed out on their foam mattresses. Heading for the door, I caught my reflection in the mirrored wardrobe and stopped, taking in the rapid transformation my body had already undergone once removed from my Washington State McDiet. I gazed at myself, as if looking at a stranger—a barefoot, wild-haired, much thinner stranger—wearing the long, satin nightgown Asya had given me a few years ago when we were still friends.

Even so early, a warm, Mediterranean breeze wafted in, blowing the sheers across the arched windows like white clouds on their way to a final, delicious swirl against my body, and for a moment, I felt good. Then I remembered Karim.

Glaring at myself, I turned from the mirror and continued to the door, reaching up on my tiptoes to grab the key I'd hidden on the doorjamb after locking us all in the room for the night. In Safa, like most Palestinian homes in the West Bank, the custom was to install individual key-locks on each door, making it theoretically possible to lock someone inside. It was an idea antithetical to my ingrained North American obsession with fire safety. But then again, so were the bars on the windows, immovable, drilled right into the stone masonry. At first, the idea of the key locks and the bars really bothered me, but now I was actually starting to appreciate them in that death-trap-waiting-to-happen house we now occupied. What better way was there to keep Karim from hurling himself down the stairwell when I wasn't looking? As for the fire danger, I tried to console myself that at least the house was made of stone.

I let myself out of the room, closed the door quietly behind me and went straight to the loveseat, pushing it until it was firmly wedged against the entrance to the stairway. It wasn't a great solution, but it would work until I could get the construction workers to close it off somehow. Satisfied, I brewed a cup of strong coffee and sat at the kitchen table staring out the window, doing my best to keep mental images of splattered babies, garage door guillotines and disco fire-traps at bay.

When the kids finally awoke, I gave them their new "usual" breakfast—mortadella, eggs fried in fragrant goat butter, fresh farmer's cheese, cracked green olives, and *za'atar*, a mix of wild thyme, oregano, salt and sesame seeds eaten with fresh, hot *taboon* bread and olive oil. Together, it gave the tongue a salty, lemony, delicious mix of oily-spicy-goodness to start the day, and it was all washed down with steaming, sweet sage tea, freshly picked from the small herb patch next to the orchard.

When we finished, I grabbed Karim and headed out and across the road to Khalid's, where he and Asya were sitting outside by a fire, simmering grapes into *dibis*, the thick, dark syrup that would be a staple during the coming winter. Deep in discussion, they barely noticed my approach, but I was sure they'd noticed his other wife, Sawsan, puttering in the adjoining field, picking sprigs of mint along with stray snippets of their conversation.

Yelling to Karim to stay away from the tick-covered dogs lounging with their puppies on the road, I cleared my throat, wishing them a good morning.

"*Sabah al khair*," I said, watching Asya prod and stoke the fire like a witch over her brew.

"*Sabah ennour*," "Morning of light." They responded in unison, as I pulled up a plastic chair just out of range of the thick column of smoke, and got straight to the point— at least, as straight as I could make it with my grammar issues.

"Karim run up stairs!" I started. "Big hole! I must go fast and I catch his foot before *death*!"

A long moment passed while they deciphered my cryptic exclamation, but their wide-eyed expressions reassured me that I'd been understood.

"*Alhamdullah!*" they exclaimed. "Thank God he's okay!"

"Yes, *Alhamdulillah*," I agreed. "'But, I wanted to ask you to…"

"You have to be more careful!" Asya interrupted. "Where were you?!"

I paused for a second, fighting the sudden urge to reach out and squeeze her neck—hard, and took in a long, slow breath. "Well, I shouldn't have to worry about him falling into a hole inside his own house, Asya. Anyway," I continued, turning to Khalid, "If you could please tell the workers to find a way to install a doorway to the stairs, and to fix the garage door...."

There, again I paused. Damn, I had no idea how to say motor or safety cut-off in Arabic. "Umm....See..." I stammered, "I want the door to stop if children are under...it must have a light that knows there are children before it kills them."

Out of the corner of my eye, I could see Asya shoot me a smirking once-over, and I cursed my pitiful vocabulary. *For God's sakes, I sounded like a flaming idiot.* No wonder she thought she could mess with me—I seemed too stupid to notice.

Sighing, I tried to explain myself again; finally mixing in some pantomime to be sure Khalid understood my meaning. Then I excused myself, removed a bulging-eyed puppy from Karim's enthusiastic embrace, and headed home, ready for my next step.

I was determined to hire a reliable baby-sitter—with or without my mother-in-law's approval—so I called Dr. Muhammad's wife, Sameeha, and asked her to arrange a meeting that evening with a possible candidate she had mentioned a few days before.

Ra'eda was an excellent choice, she told me. Not only did she really need the work, but she was from outside the tribe, and was an educated townie from Beit Ommar. All of these points raised the odds that she would actually take on the job. The problem was domestic work is highly regarded in Palestinian culture, but getting paid for it is not. I didn't understand the rationale, but it meant that finding someone to babysit for pay from the village itself was well-nigh impossible. Still, I could see Grandma wasn't up to the task, whether or not she insisted she was, so while she may not have intentionally sabotaged my first day by disappearing, I was now forewarned not to take any more chances.

Unfortunately, news spreads as fast in Safa as if it were carried on the wind—and there, the weather 'tis mighty blustery. That meant when evening came, so did my mother-in-law, trailed by the evil sisters-in-law like some kind of anti-babysitter posse. Obviously aware of my plan to bring in an "outsider," they settled on the sofas in the living room, watching and whispering to each other as I continued to scurry around readying the house for my meeting, growing more sweaty and flustered by the moment.

Doing my best to ignore them, I busied myself filling the ridiculous gilded tissue box (*de rigueur* salon décor in the village), moving the nested tea tables into place, and bringing out plates of cookies and the tea glasses and readying the demitasse coffee service for my visitor, all the while mentally rehearsing Arabic responses to the verbal onslaught I knew would start any moment.

Unable to contain herself any longer, my mother-in-law called me back from the kitchen, where I was starting the fresh mint tea.

"Who are you bringing here?" she demanded. "I told you I would take care of the children."

"*Amtee*," I responded, "I know you would, but it's too much work for you. Besides, Ahmad told me that I should find someone to help out when I'm not at home, and the house is dangerous…"

"But she will be expensive!" she interrupted, closing one eye and wagging her finger at me. "Besides, you already paid the workers too much money, and now you want a new door, too! Where will Ahmad find all this money!"

I flashed Asya a quick glare.

"But Ahmad wants it," I said, using my husband's wishes as an immutable defense, "What can I do?" putting up my hands helplessly, as if a babysitter was the last thing on earth I wanted myself.

I excused myself to bring in the tray of tea, passing it to each woman in order of their age. When I reached Asya, second to last, she took her glass and blew on its surface, cooling the searing hot liquid and sending sprigs of Sawsan's mint swirling: a bright green tempest in her cup.

Having given up hope that the women would leave before getting a look at "the girl," I resigned myself to sitting down and waiting with them, willfully ignoring my mother-in-law's continuing lament over my wretched excess.

When Ra'eda finally made her entrance—more than an hour late— she was dressed in the West Bank equivalent of business attire: knee length polyester blazer, slacks, pointy high heels, sequined white headscarf and intricate make-up. She exuded an attitude of superiority that immediately put me off. In fact, from the moment she arrived, she gave the impression that it was I who was applying for the privilege of employing her, deflected my questions, and generally came across as a stuck-up sourpuss. I couldn't stand her, and that was even before she began talking to my sister-in-laws about me, since I was obviously too clueless to understand the discussion.

"Well, she does speak some Arabic, doesn't she?" she asked, "Does she really pray? And her kids, poor things, don't they speak any Arabic at all?"

By the time she finally left, telling me she would "think about" the job, I was furious. There was no way in hell I would hire such a dour, nosy bitch of a woman—an opinion, by the way, my sister-in-laws shared. Their negative assessments also included the breadth of her ass, the shade of her skin, and her city accent. It was actually one of the first times I was tempted to agree with them.

My "poor kids," indeed! I certainly had no intention of calling her back. That's why I was so surprised the next morning when she suddenly showed up for work.

I was hanging laundry on the line between the columns on the orchard veranda, clipping my bras and underwear underneath T-shirts and towels as I'd been instructed for "modesty's sake," when I heard footsteps behind me. Turning, I was shocked to see Ra'eda, in all ways a very different person than the night before. Sans makeup and in work clothes, she told me that she was happy to have met me, that she wanted the job very much, and that she'd only acted aloof for the benefit of the other women in the room. She actually smiled!

"I only have one request," she said. "Please, if you could just tell your mother and sisters-in-law that you decided to hire me to teach the children Arabic, and don't tell them if I cook or clean anything…I don't want them to say I'm a maid."

I agreed, still a little wary, but disarmed by her abrupt personality change. The truth was, she was the best option I had. Besides, I knew she would do a good job because my mother-in-law wouldn't be able to stop herself from checking in on her all day. After all, someone would have to make sure that her son was getting his money's worth. Heck, maybe she'd be so focused on the babysitter that she'd lay off my faults for a while. Yes, I thought. This might work out after all.

CHAPTER 12

What Would Solomon Do?

Instinct is the nose of the mind.

-Madame De Girardin

Although some things seemed to be coming together— I liked my job, my students seemed to like me, and I was slowly figuring out the daily details of life in the West Bank, the kids were a different story. In fact, by the time the heat of mid-July hit its zenith, so did their homesickness. It was almost two full months since our arrival, and Ibrahim and Amani were both miserable.

Karim was too young to know the difference, but Ibrahim and Amani were fed up with the constant visitors, or "invasions," as Amani put it, which were the norm in the village. If they were lonely in America, there was no such thing in Safa, where no one discusses having the necessity of "calling ahead," or even knocking, for that matter. In fact, it was common for me to suddenly turn around to find someone standing behind me.

Almost as bad, if the door was locked—a rare occurrence, with the kids coming in and out all day—the would-be visitor simply climbed the barred windows, popped their head in, and yelled until I answered. I couldn't even pretend that I wasn't at home unless I was willing, and sometimes I was, to hide behind walls or crawl across the floor to stay out of sight.

In addition to the constant company, the kids hated other things about village life, foremost among them Safa's lack of Xboxes, cable TV, "real toys" and the English language. Amani, in particular, was so frustrated by her cousins' inability to grasp *her* inability to understand their Arabic (and that exponential increases in volume were not helpful), that she would often break into tears and run away from them, locking herself in her room.

But the worst moment had to be the morning I awoke to news that Ibrahim had packed his suitcase (including such useful items as his Power Rangers action figures, DVDs and a few cans of Pepsi), and run away while I slept. Thankfully, his uncle happened upon him as he neared the outskirts of the village, striding along, rolling suitcase in tow, determined to walk all the way back to America.

It was at that moment that I realized I'd have to work harder to make the place more of a home for them (well, that and the fact there seemed to be some serious holes in Ibrahim's geography skills needing attention). Sure, I was doing a lot of running around working my stuff out, but Ibrahim and Amani needed a break from the village, too, as much as they needed to somehow believe the place could be fun.

Unfortunately, the West Bank isn't exactly associated with either fun or entertainment, so after giving it some thought, I decided that the best approach would be something like a hippie-type home-schooling program of bonding with the ol'homeland. After all, I'd dragged them here. It was time they started to identify with the place, the history, the religion—this place was just full of religion! I would make this a year they'd never forget, and by the end of it they would be the youngest experts on *Terra Sancta* around. I decided then that the first step on my new agenda should involve an outing to the hands-down coolest place this side of Jerusalem—Solomon's Pools.

I'd visited the pools, known locally as *Buraik Solayman*, shortly after my wedding thirteen years before, and I remembered the place as much for its historical origins as for its beauty. Made up of three open reservoirs, each more than a football field in length and up to fifty feet deep, Solomon's Pools nestled in stepped formation in the middle of a vast, wooded valley just outside of Bethlehem. Legend said they were built by King Solomon and a legion of spirits and demons placed under his power by God, but most historians agreed that the pools were actually built by King Herod during the Second Temple period.

Whatever their origins, the place represented an amazing technological feat in that era, serving the Temple Mount in distant Jerusalem with an uninterrupted supply of fresh water via a series of gently sloping aqueducts, portions of which remain.

It was the place's more recent history that I knew would spark the kids' imagination, though, for today Solomon's Pools are associated with the hundreds of drownings that have happened there over the years. Apparently, victims were pulled down under the green water's surface, never to be seen again. Although I tended to believe the culprit was the long swamp weeds growing from the pools' murky depths, I knew that the kids (*Goosebumps* series aficionados) would be fascinated by the story. Also, since the pools were now almost completely drained by the Palestinian Authority, presumably to prevent more tragedies, the kids wouldn't be in danger of falling prey to the site's mysterious curse.

The drive to the pools covered a winding road that snaked past two refugee camps, a large settlement bloc, and some of the most beautiful countryside in the Holy Land. As we drove, we opened the windows and car roof and blasted the latest Arabic pop song "Girl in a Short Skirt" as we whizzed past old, abandoned houses dotting the roadside, miles of vineyards, stepped fields, and stone fences. We were forced to slow occasionally on the way to pass donkeys laden with firewood and piles of grape leaves, shepherds driving their sheep between the fields, and even the occasional camel loping along, looking bored with the world. The kids seemed to brighten with every passing mile.

When we finally pulled off the pavement of the main highway and onto the mud-baked road leading to the pools, the kids' collective intake of breath and loud "Wow!!!" told me that the spot would be a hit. There, in front of my dusty windshield, we could see the first pool stretching out as if it had been carved from the earth by God Himself, adorned with blocks of stone as big as a car stacked down inside like giant stairs, beckoning the kids to come and explore.

Best yet, though, was the fact that in spite of the place's historic importance, it was virtually deserted—deemed too dangerous for typical tourists after a series of politically motivated knife attacks upon Israeli settlers in the area, and declared legally off-limits to Israeli civilians (the military could go wherever they wanted, however) because of the area's designation by the Israeli government as a Palestinian autonomous zone. This meant the kids could play as if the place was their own private playground.

I was happy to see that they took full advantage of the situation, sliding down the pool's sloping sides, walking along the ruined aqueducts, and picking up broken shards of pottery and ancient jug-handles for their "collections." They even found a dark stone shaft in the hillside leading into a hidden, underground passageway, and I promised them that next time we'd come back with a rope so I could climb down and find out what was inside. They were thrilled, and I, for a moment, got to feel like Supermom.

The magic of the place seemed to be a charm for us all, and that day marked a kind of turning point. Although it was still taking some time for them to adjust, Amani and Ibrahim's smiles returned—especially when I found a store in Hebron where they carried some of their favorite snacks from America—including Twinkies!—which they took pride in introducing to their cousins.

Soon they were playing soccer in the road, making up games, and climbing trees with their cousins instead of avoiding them, and showing off their favorite cartoons from their American DVD collections—which the kids loved, even if they couldn't understand the dialogue.

So, too, their cousins showed them their games, shared their favorite snacks, and even tried to defend their young American visitors from me and anyone else they happened to cross when they were misbehaving. Soon Ibrahim and Amani were picking up Arabic at a rapid pace, their cousins in turn learning almost as many words from them in English. No doubt about it, we were all finally settling in, something we celebrated by decorating the first floor of the house with off-season Christmas lights, revamped in the market as flashing star and crescents for the upcoming Ramadan holiday.

Even our excessive visitor problem seemed to ease a bit after I figured out that if I visited family and neighbors more often in their homes, they would come less often to mine! In fact, it was during one of these visits at our doctor relative's home for a delicious dinner of stuffed grape leaves, fresh roasted chicken, and French fries—ah, I loved Sameeha and the doctor—that another guest (one of the legion of middle-aged, advice-spouting male cousins) informed me that it was a "very bad idea" to take my kids outside Safa.

According to him, my yellow-plated car put us at risk from the Palestinian locals, should they take a notion to stone us. Further, my Palestinian appearance might provoke the nearby Jewish settlers, who had, um…guns—especially if I used "their" roads while out and about. According to him, Safa was the only safe place to be.

It was a frustrating predicament. Clearly, he was right on some level, and I wasn't so naive as to think the West Bank was just like home in Washington. Still, the more time I spent with the family in the village, the more I noticed that their years of rural isolation may have warped their perspective a bit. After all, at first they'd told me that my car might be stoned in the neighboring town, Beit Ommar, but I hadn't had problems there, in Hebron, or in any of the smaller neighboring villages.

But the man had a point, and rare as they might be, attacks did happen. I had to be careful, but I couldn't exactly keep the kids in the house all the time. Although I couldn't deny that his advice had rattled me, I sensed that I would have to find a balance on my own.

Thanking Sameeha for the dinner, the kids and I headed outside for the short walk home, under a shining moon that more than made up for the lack of street lights. I carried Karim, who had fallen into a fast sleep, and our footfalls crunched on the rocky path, answering the cricket-song that seemed to echo from every direction.

Walking along, I felt a simple, contented peace that I hadn't felt for the longest time—and surely never in downtown Seattle at night. We were much safer here, I thought, especially in tiny Safa. It was all a matter of weighing risk in a calm and logical way.

Nearing home, we passed out of the glow of distant city lights, glittering from across the hills and into the shadow of our house, dark and seemingly ready for sleep as we were. Even the crickets seemed to quiet down. It was only when we rounded the corner and were face to face with the Israeli Army unit crouching in my driveway that I realized sleep wouldn't come easily that night.

CHAPTER 13

Tribal Life, Ta'mre Style

We should manage our fortune as we do our health—enjoy
it when good, be patient when it is bad, and never apply
violent remedies except in an extreme necessity

-François de la Rochefoucauld

e stared at each other in a moment of shocked silence—me, my three kids, and them—five men in black greasepaint, mushroom-like camouflage caps and night vision goggles. *Why the hell are they in my driveway?* Then, without a word, we walked past each other, they striding by us into the night—and us into the house for a fitful night's sleep

When I woke the next morning, I made for Huda's and told them about the patrol (over some of her delicious, hot, homemade bread), but I was surprised to hear that, according to them, it was *"adee,"* an Arabic word that meant "normal" almost always, as in, "Oh, that shit?! Yeah, its *adee.*"

Oh. Okay...

I had no choice but to try to take their comfort with the status quo as a good sign, even though my husband said that when he was growing up in Safa he almost never saw the military. Well, apparently, it was *adee* now. A couple of days later, though, I learned that the military might not be the only thing I should worry about in the village.

It was a beautiful, sunny afternoon, and I was just about to settle into a nice, little nap when Amani and a group of her cousins burst into the house in a panic. Panting and wide-eyed, the girls unleashed a flood of Arabic that I couldn't understand until Amani finally caught her breath enough to tell me that there was a huge fight outside, complete with "sticks and lots of blood."

Having no idea what she could be talking about—soldiers, criminals, kids, what? I ran outside where I saw a crowd surrounding two Red Crescent ambulances (the Middle Eastern version of the Red Cross), their medics loading four bloody men onto boards. It was mayhem, and everyone seemed to be upset and running around. More and more people gathered between the houses until the crowd started to resemble a mob—complete with—no kidding—people brandishing clubs.

Everyone was shouting, and many of them seemed to be teetering on the verge of hysteria, but I couldn't understand anything. Then I found Huda and her daughter, Manar, among the mass of women who were also gathered, and they explained in slower, simpler Arabic that four men from "our tribe" had been attacked in the neighboring town. The crowd, the clubs and the shouting were all part of the beginnings of a *tosha*; a tribal battle that could morph into an outright "war."

Although I knew Palestine was a tribal society, and I'd heard that the Ta'mre tribe that my husband's family belonged to was notorious for their ferocity, I always assumed actual tribal battles were a remote possibility. I certainly didn't expect to actually see a clash in front of me. But in the West Bank, where local laws are still hit or miss, and police are scarce and unreliable at best, having a tribe behind you can offer a kind of protection. The fiercer one's tribe is, the less likely anyone else will mess with you.

In general, actual tribal fights were rare in the area because the eck Out Receipt

g Harbor Library
3-548-3305
v.piercecountylibrary.org

iday, September 23, 2016 12:14:01 PM
325

em: 39093080513377
tle: The wisdom of the Beguines : the fo
otten story of a medieval women's moveme

e: 10/14/2016

em: 39093080022312
tle: The cross and the lynching tree
e: 10/14/2016

em: 39093066724477
tle: All roads lead to Jerusalem : an Am
ican Muslim mom's search for meaning in
e Holy Land
e: 10/14/2016

tal items: 3

ols for Students
line homework help for grades K-12
ve tutors, science experiments
lpful databases and lots more.
sit tools.pcls.us

Ta'mre had several thousand members and strong organization. All it took was one phone call to the *Mukhtar*, or chief, to bring out the rest of the tribe, which would descend like locusts from dozens of neighboring communities in and around Bethlehem. Because of this, people mostly stayed on their good behavior.

Today, though, because a pair of hot-headed brothers had decided to take their chances and attack the four men (now headed to the hospital) for some trivial slight in town, and because the brothers were from a rival tribe, their entire clan and home town could face "our" wrath. It was crazy, Wild West stuff. Still, the thought that *this is my kids' tribe* occurred to me, and I realized that I was oddly pleased at the notion.

CHAPTER 14

Take the Heat

And finally Winter, with its bitin', whinin' wind,
and all the land will be mantled with snow.

-ROY BEAN

After the ambulances left for the hospital, everyone cleared out of the road while they waited for a tribal council meeting at the home of the injured men to decide how to proceed. Although the village women weren't directly involved in the meeting, children stationed at the open windows and doorways ferried the news to the rest of us, waiting in our homes to see what would happen next.

According to the reports, many tribal members had argued for a full-on assault involving the entire tribe, but thankfully, calmer heads prevailed. Instead, the parties settled on what was called an *atwah*, in this case a three-day cooling-off period during which both sides agreed to monetary compensation in lieu of battle, and everyone was relieved because people died in these kinds of situations every year. In fact, my mother-in-law's first husband (Dr. Muhammad's father) had been killed in a fight similar to this one. Thankfully, though, this time the clubs were stowed away; the attackers' families were safe again, and we could go to the grocery store, which was on the opposing tribe's turf, without fear of an attack. I could still get my nefarious Pepsi fix and nobody died. Who could ask for more?

Happily, the next weeks went calmly; there weren't any more fights, and I didn't see any more soldiers in my driveway. The children's cousins started school—all cute in their striped uniforms—and Amani even convinced me to let her try out fourth grade instead of home school. But when I went with her to her first class, we entered the classroom just in time to see the pretty, gentle- looking teacher smack the hell out of a doll-like little girl in pigtails for forgetting her notebook at home. It was Amani's first and last day at school.

The construction workers had finally finished the garage, electricity and the stairs, and were then focused on finishing up installing the heating system before winter set in, hoisting the large, industrial looking boiler and fuel tank up to the roof to connect it to the radiators below.

Although the cooking routine remained under control, thanks to Huda's daughters and the babysitter, who covered for me on the days I had to work, I was looking forward to the day the house would just be finished already and the workers gone. I'd been troubled by the persistent feeling that I owed them more than the money we were paying them—nothing sexual, of course, but the feeling that they must be taken care of—water, tea, food…Somehow I never felt that I did enough for them, perhaps a feeling mirrored from my on-hold marriage. It was this feeling that I needed to take care of the needs of men *because* they were men…(after all, Ra'eda didn't expect me to make her lunch every day) filled me with a bitterness disproportionate to the actual effort required of me, as if I'd somehow overdosed on "feminine domesticity" pills.

It didn't help that the workers were completely incompetent. Unfortunately, it was only after they'd accidentally flooded the house with hundreds of gallons of dirty water that they admitted the important fact that they'd never actually worked on radiators before. They did finish the project, eventually, though, and although by the end we'd shelled out a cool 15,000 dollars, I felt relieved, especially as the first cold evenings set in and Khalid finally set about teaching me how to fire up the thing.

We both trudged up to the fourth floor where the boiler sat in all its glory, flanked by a tank of diesel as big as my car, and a quarter full. The smell up here was heavenly—a mixture of curing cement, wet rebar, seeping fuel and fire, and I breathed it in as deeply as I could without looking like a huffer. Interrupting me from my olfactory reverie, Khalid explained that once I flipped the "big switch" downstairs, all I had to do was come up, make sure that the tank was open to the boiler, and push the start button. That was it.

Okay, I thought. *Easy enough.* I tried it, and sure enough, there was a satisfying whoosh of the ignition, and the boiler's round window flashed white, then red, its roaring inferno pushing blessed heat into the rooms below. Let there be warmth!

And on that night, there was. On the second and third, too. However, when the chill of the fourth night descended, something was wrong. I flipped the "big switch," and nothing. No satisfying tick-tick-tick of the radiators accepting water and steam.

I started to pray.

Putting on a pair of flip-flops and a jacket, I grabbed the flashlight and crunched up the cement and rebar ramps leading up to the roof. When I got there, however, the boiler—shiny, awesome, expensive—was dark and silent. I reached down and pushed its own start button, just as Khalid had shown me. Still nothing. *Shit,* I thought. *I'll have to tell Khalid it's broken…* As I turned to leave, though, my flashlight glinted on the fuel gage. Empty. Two thousand Shekels (more than five hundred dollars) had lasted for exactly three nights of heat for what amounted to a small, two-bedroom space. I might as well burn the money bill by bill.

I told Khalid about the problem the next day, expecting him to find a leak, a diesel thief, something wrong. After he and his friend Omar poked around awhile upstairs, however, the only suggestion they could come up with was that I should seal off half of the radiators to conserve heat. Conserve? How could it be possible to burn through what must have been hundreds of liters of diesel in just three nights?

I was frustrated and worried. On one hand, I noticed a definite tone in Khalid's and Omar's voices, a look between them as if I'd somehow managed—probably due to a mixture of womanly stupidity and foreign decadence—to consume more fuel than a semi on a cross-country haul. What the hell?! I doubted that it was even possible to use that much heat, even if I'd turned the entire first floor into a sauna. But the fact that they weren't considering that there must be a mechanical problem or a leak in the system made me suspect that there might be a thief somewhere in the system, perhaps siphoning fuel from the long line leading up to the tank and that was a scary thought. Plus, there was the pressing problem that the weather was by then getting seriously cold.

Still not budging on their assessment of the problem, and without any modifications on the heating system that I could see, they called for the diesel truck to pump up more fuel to the tank, trickles dripping from the makeshift coupling outside the front door. It was a problem, particularly because I had to shell out another two thousand shekels, which left me with a mere three hundred for the rest of the week (about eighty dollars). For a family of four, that was stretching it.

Three days later, with half the radiators shut off, the tank was empty again, this time the problem vaguely chalked up to some kind of miscalculation; some mysterious incompatibility of house and design that made the boiler completely useless (unless I was willing to spend two thousand Shekels every three days all winter long).

When the real cold came the following week, I closed off all of the first floor's rooms except the kitchen, bathroom, and family room, and hung heavy blankets over the house's inside arches to make a single, heatable space, and fired up one of the locally produced space heaters, known as a *soba*. This was little more than a hollow metal box containing a propane tank and a hose, faced with a large, exposed vertical burner, but it really cranked out the heat. I'd just have to forget the fact that it was also dangerous as hell.

Still, it was better than freezing, and I just happened to have brought along a carbon monoxide detector from America (an unexpected benefit of my obsessive "what-if" packing philosophy). All I could do was try to forget that we'd just wasted $15,000, although I did find it odd that my husband's family members weren't as horrified as me by the waste. Still, then again I sensed that there was an unspoken assumption that I had unlimited money to burn—which certainly wasn't the case. Regardless, I tried to be grateful that we were at least warm and comfortable, and as we all slept, spread out on our mattresses under the fiery glow of the soba, in our now, one room home (for the rest of the winter anyway), I realized I was.

Part Three

Small Battles on the Road

CHAPTER 15

Off-Limits

Curiosity does, no less than devotion, pilgrims make.

-Abraham Cowley

In travel books, the Holy Land often seems like the back lot of a Universal Studios guest tour. X would mark the spots where Abraham prepared to sacrifice his son, King Herod slew the innocents, Jesus' first fell on his way to his Crucifixion, the stone from whence Muhammad rose to heaven....

If you are a history buff, or of a religious bent, being here can bring about something close to a compulsion to see every single site, to hit the "God trail" and get in as many prayers as you can. I suspect it's a feeling that many spiritual pilgrims have shared over the centuries, although I wasn't exactly a pilgrim. I now lived here, and that meant that I had to learn to pace myself as a local should. It was something that rarely affected true locals—this manic attraction to the "holy sites"—but almost always appeared in transplants like myself, whether Jewish, Muslim or Christian. There was even a name for the disorder in its most extreme form: "Jerusalem Syndrome."

In clinical terms, Jerusalem Syndrome is a manifestation of delusions or obsessions, even psychoses triggered by Jerusalem (and the rest of the Holy Land) that has been known to affect religious travelers of all faiths. These pilgrims, although "previously balanced," somehow came unhinged in the Holy Land, believing they heard the voice of God, saw angels, or *were* Jesus, Moses, or another religious figure—in fact, one man, Denis Rohan, an Australian Christian afflicted with the syndrome, could have started World War III when he, believing he was the Lord's "emissary," tried to burn down the Aqsa Mosque in 1969, in order to pave the way for the second coming of Jesus.

I personally had no desire to burn anything, nor did I fancy myself Sarah, or Esther, or Mary, but I did itch to see, be in, and feel holy sites as often and obsessively as a sex-starved Saudi let loose in Amsterdam's red-light district. In truth, I didn't even care about the religious ownership of the place (after all, Judaism, Christianity and Islam all sprang from the same origin: here, anyway). I prayed in the Temple Mount's Dome of the Rock, the famous golden-domed building that has become the symbol of the city and is the third holiest place in Islam, visited the Church of the Holy Sepulchre, where Christians believe Jesus was crucified, and the Nativity where he was born—I'm even one of the few Muslims I've ever seen at the Western Wall. I would even go so far as to say my fascination, my own form of "Jerusalem Syndrome" was behind my attraction to the places that really began to draw me in with each passing week: the places that were off-limits, guarded, forgotten, or somehow forbidden.

Admittedly, part of my urge to go off-limits has to do with a natural attraction to the mysterious. I would wager that this urge is a part of many people's attraction to ghost hunting, a yearning for that which reminds the soul that there may well be other dimensions—a search for confirmation that God really exists. And although there are plenty sites with legends, and accounts of the miraculous in and around the Holy Land, there are some that are considered so holy that they are a point of jealous contention among the people who live there. From secret tunnels, to underground chambers, and streets that once ran with blood up to the knees of Crusader horses—these places are closed not only to tourists, but to locals as well. Maybe it was my own quirky manifestation of Jerusalem Syndrome, but when I learned of these places, I desperately wanted in.

Although I couldn't completely explain what really motivated my attraction to some of these places—I knew that it was something more than mere curiosity. Most likely, it was a mixture of my old urge to be accepted (after all, I would have to prove myself somehow to the authorities in charge of the closed sites) as well as the urge to somehow push my limits during the limited time I had there on my own. Whatever the reason, something smacking of obsession began to grow in my heart. And now that I was here without my husband, without a man, without a friend or companion, it was an urge that I could actually try to satisfy completely on my own merits.

By now, it was fewer than five months into our stay and I'd visited several places that neither my husband nor anyone in the family had ever seen. This was no small thing given that the territories of Palestine and Israel, combined, equal less than ten thousand square miles (slightly larger than the state of New Jersey), and was the nomadic home turf of the family for at least ten generations. Yet the truth was, I couldn't have seen most of them with my husband even if he wanted to, either because he wouldn't be allowed to go as a Palestinian, because many of the sites were "inappropriate" by his family's standards, or because going to see them was just plain risky, and I would feel responsible if anything happened to him—or anyone else I dragged along.

On and off through the centuries, and certainly for the last sixty-four years, the Holy Land has been as divided as Southern California gang territory. Opposing factions don't visit each other's turf unless armed with a gun and backed up by an army unit. Palestinians from the West Bank and Gaza (especially men) are not allowed to visit Israeli areas (except sometimes as laborers), and Israeli Jews would never enter a Palestinian village except by (sometimes fatal) mistake, or as part of an armed military operation. In fact, large red signs printed in English and Hebrew are posted outside literally every Palestinian city, town, and village throughout the occupied territories, warning Israeli drivers against making any wrong turns.

One of the things I was happy to discover, however, was that the head scarf and conservative dress I always wore meant that I could pretty well pass as in Arab in Palestinian areas (until I opened my mouth), and be virtually ignored as a (relatively) harmless woman in most Jewish areas. Also, as a visa-holding American, I could and often did pull the clueless tourist card—which certainly wasn't a stretch—and pretend to be lost. This blending-in afforded me a great opportunity to see the places I'd always wanted to, and since my husband wasn't around, I didn't have to tell anyone where I was going. Sure, it might be a little dangerous sometimes—if anything happened to me in those places, nobody would even know where to begin looking for me! However, I decided that for the time being, the risk didn't bother me as much as provoking the ire of my in-laws or my husband.

With that in mind, one afternoon I decided to give it a try. I called home and made sure that the babysitter was comfortably in charge of Karim (by then the older ones spent almost all of their waking hours outside roaming the village with their cousins), and I drove to Jerusalem after work, passing through the tunnels into the Gilo neighborhood. The Gilo Road is simply the fastest way to Jerusalem, *if* you are an Israeli or a "tourist" like me. It was also infamous because it was one of the most impressive roadways in terms of scale and money spent, and the most blatantly unfair to the Palestinians, who were forbidden from using it, even though it was constructed on the Palestinian side of the Green Line. In fact, it was this stretch of highway that really brought the whole issue of "apartheid roads" to the world's attention. These roads and high-ways connected the more than two hundred Israeli settlements inside the West Bank to the rest of Israel. Even former President Jimmy Carter, the architect of the historic Camp David Peace Accord, described the roads like the Gilo tunnels as "spider webs," noting that not only were the Palestinians restricted from using the roads, but in many cases, even from crossing them.

Of course, since I had my yellow-plated car and my tourist visa, I was usually allowed onto the road (although sometimes individual soldiers would turn me away). Still, that didn't mean that I could just drive on through the large checkpoint in front of the tunnels like the settlers and other Israelis (although dark-skinned Jews without typical settler garb might have to slow down to show their IDs, which, in Israel, indicate re-ligion). This was because whether Israeli citizens or not, all Palestinians, Christian or Muslim, as well as many Israelis of Middle Eastern heritage, *always* had to pull over in a designated side lane to be inspected, while their Jewish cousins sped by with nary a break-tap. Because my head scarf made me "look Arab" to the soldiers manning the lanes, that meant me, too.

It was here that I regularly got a good lesson on just how insulated many young Israelis were (and at the Gilo checkpoint, they were almost always the youngest soldiers, right out of high school), especially about Muslims. For many, if not all of the soldiers, I was the first non-Arab Muslim they'd ever seen. And in spite of the fact that the majority of Muslims in the world aren't Arabs, I could just not get them to grasp what "kind of person" I was, even after I showed them my American passport. That was until I learned to say the magic line, "I'm an *Ameri-can-American*, you know…*American*?"

For some crazy reason that would usually explain it all.

Beseder…ah, it's all good. Go ahead.

And I (courtesy of American-American) was off.

∞

As you emerge from the Gilo tunnels and approach Jerusalem from the south, you pass a large "Entering Jerusalem" sign that, at first glance, looks just like any other highway sign in the world, except that it it's trilingual. "Welcome to Jerusalem," it proclaims in English, then Hebrew, and finally Arabic. Seems egalitarian as heck as long as you can't actually read it.

Thus, it read, on the final line, "Ahlan Wa Sahlan fi *Yerushalyim*"—all Arabic right up to the name of the city, where its Hebrew name is then rendered in bold, oddly connected Arabic script. Strange, given the Arabic word for the city is Al Quds, and has been for thousands of years. That the English version got to keep its "Jerusalem," and the Hebrew its "Yerushalyim" while the Arabic version had its traditional name replaced said a lot, and was designed to be a virtual slap to the face of every Palestinian who could read it. Of course, if you were one of the many tourists passing by, it looked innocent enough, but the locals on both sides knew the score in the Holy Land—where even something as innocuous as a highway sign becomes a metaphor for the Israeli/Palestinian conflict—there for all to see in stark, reflective paint.

Although I told the family that I was planning to pray in the Dome of the Rock and do some clothes shopping (oddly, the clothes shopping was by far the better-received itinerary explanation), I was actually planning to visit two places—both pools—before nightfall, and because it was winter I didn't have much time. Still, before I could park my car and head for the first pool in the Old City, I had to make a pit-stop to buy some pepper spray in the New City's Ben Yehuda market, where I had spotted some in a shop a few weeks before.

Ben Yehuda market, located in downtown Jerusalem, is an odd place—a mishmash of artsy Judaica shops, cheap clothes, gelato and—what else—army surplus stores, all selling cheap "IDF" T-shirts and used flak jackets, some still sporting the word "PRESS" spelled out in black permanent marker on sports tape. They also sold pepper spray, and I needed it for some of the places I was planning to go.

With newly purchased spray in hand, I drove again through the time warp that separates West Jerusalem from her eastern side, and dropped abruptly from the modern, busy thoroughfare onto the narrow roads that snaked through the neighborhoods next to the Old City walls. It was here that the city offered the best view...the one that could really take your breath away. Otherwise, the road was very distracting, with its construction, dirt, traffic, and darting pedestrians, The Old City and its Golden Dome seem to appear to have sprung up from the dank earth like some fantastical scene in a pop-up book.

At the end of the road I finally parked in the tiny asphalt parking lot outside of the Damascus Gate, known in Arabic as *Bab al Amud*, or the "Gate of the Column." It was named after the Roman victory column that stood there until the second century CE. Today, the column is long gone, but if you look up at the fortified, castle-like structure, you can usually see its modern equivalent—an Israeli soldier lounging in the large, stone rampart window above the gate, gun against the wall, one knee up, like a pirate in a Captain Morgan commercial.

Just inside, too, waited omnipresent blue-uniformed policemen, scanning the crowd for young men who might be there without the "tasreeh," the permission they needed to be in Jerusalem. But even here, the Jerusalem of the imagination asserted its age-old grip on the place—and you couldn't help but feel that once you'd passed through the gate's massive, rotting door you had passed back into history. You might be accompanied, however, by a mob pushing through the bottleneck that the gate was designed to create (a remnant of the centuries the wall served as protection during war or siege). Many of them looked just as they might have a hundred years ago—from Haredi Jews, priests and nuns of every Christian denomination, Muslim women, and old-time Palestinian men who looked as if they'd just stepped out of the pages of *Lawrence of Arabia*. Then, just when you thought you were smack dab in a genuine, Jerusalem moment, you'd pass through the arch on the other side and back into the sun, suddenly faced with a vista of shops, kiosks, and tables displaying scarves, plastic toys and—what else—crotchless body suits.

And this was where all of the fun was. For here, innocuous-looking smooth stone pushcart ramps were one of the few ways forward into the two alleyways snaking into the old quarters of the city, and unless you'd already learned that it was better to take the narrow, irregular stairs alongside, you could easily learn the hard way just how slippery those ramps could be. Later, this would become one of my favorite parts of the city, where I could sit back and watch the show with a nice, cold Pepsi in hand. It was literally a demolition derby of pushcarts, tractors, old ladies, and hapless tourists.

In fact, if you were really lucky, there might be a load of some messy fruit involved—say, watermelon—(Oh yes, it happened, and it was *mwaah*, a magnificent sight). Still, in those early days of my Jerusalem wanderings, I remained far too entranced by the otherworldliness of the place to take sick pleasure in the sight of overturned carts of watermelon bowling down pedestrians. It was a magical scene of stone and battlements, and sounds of ancient languages. Even the smell was heavenly: a combination of smoky, roasting, garlicky meat from the sandwich shop at the head of the two alleys, and fragrant piles of bright-green mint and sage, warming under the Jerusalem sun.

All of this was a siren song of the Old City, saying, "Come on in, dearie" as it pulled the faithful down into its darkened arteries and into the heart of its world.

CHAPTER 16

Troubled Waters

I'll walk where my own nature would be leading;
it vexes me to choose another guide.

-EMILY BRONTE

The road to Bethesda, part of the Via Delarosa, or the path that many Christians believe Jesus walked to his crucifixion, is bare compared to the rest of the Old City. One of the few roads wide enough to allow a car to pass, its swath of open sky makes it seem lighter. In addition, because the road is surrounded mainly by churches and homes hidden behind the road's high stone walls, it lacks the commercial feel and the mess of the rest of the Old City, somehow keeping itself a quiet haven, pretty in its cobblestones and arches.

Bethesda itself has been known since pagan times for its miraculous waters. I'd always wanted to see it, and I knew it was touristy enough to be a comfortable first step into what was fast resembling some kind of pilgrim's "to do" list pulling me forward. Plus, when you looked up the place online, it was beautiful.

An immense, walled complex deep in the Muslim Quarter north of the Temple Mount, Bethesda is essentially a huge garden. A miracle in its own right in this arid city, it must have been peerlessly breathtaking in its day. Graced by the beautiful Church of St. Anne, a twelfth century

Crusader church commemorating the birthplace of the Mother of Mary, sacred to Christians, Jews, and pagans before them, believers have come here for centuries to be relieved of their afflictions, believing that the water in the Bethesda Pool could cure them. According to the Bible:

> ...Now there is at Jerusalem by the sheep market a pool, which is called in the Hebrew tongue Bethesda, having five porches. In these lay a great multitude of impotent folk, of blind, halt, withered, waiting for the moving of the water. For an angel went down at a certain season into the pool, and troubled the water: whosoever then first after the troubling of the water stepped in was made whole of whatsoever disease he had...
>
> - John 5:1-9

Today there are no throngs of the wretched lining its pools and colonnades—although it is said that some of their spirits remain (no matter, you'd never catch me hanging around the place at night). But there are lots of hushed, orderly tourists wearing matching sun visors emblazoned with their tour group's logo.

Darting between them, I stepped through the old fortified door frame and was surprised, despite having seen its picture, by its openness: the beautiful courtyard, field of pools, arched cisterns and ruins spread out under the watchful shadow of the church.

Although I longed to be ignored enough to just wander around and soak up the atmosphere of the place, one look around told me that I was too out-of-place for that to fly. Worse, the Christian crowds were thinning out, making me stick out even more like a sore thumb in my Islamic dress. And that's when Luigi spotted me.

Luigi—that was the name that instantly came to mind when I saw him coming my way—was all confused expression, pudgy belly, and blue denim overalls. He turned out to be the Palestinian caretaker/tour guide/gardener of the place, and he was clearly befuddled when I told him I wasn't lost, as he initially supposed.

"But, do you need help with something?" he pressed in Arabic, unable to understand what an Palestinian-Muslim woman would be doing alone in Christian Bethesda.

"No," I responded, "I just want to look around."

"Sure, welcome!" he said, a little too enthusiastically. "Actually, wait over there and I'll show you everything."

I sat down on a wide, stone bench on the broad, tree-lined lane in front of the church and watched Luigi sell tickets to a small group of European-looking tourists before he sneaked me in for a behind-the-scenes tour. We even went down into a dark, dank cistern, where he joked about the crazy foreigners and their habit of throwing money into the water in hopes of a blessing. Jerking his head to indicate the tourists walking around above us, he continued, "They throw in money. Even paper bills! The water goes up and down in here, and it used to more, before...but as soon as the tourists leave, the local boys come in and swim through that dirty water to take the money. They're poor, and the money helps them, right? Who's to say it's wrong?"

When we finished the tour of the site and its impressive gardens, Luigi (by then, he'd told me his name was Majid, but I somehow couldn't make the mental switch) seemed like an okay guy after all. He was simply a hospitable man, taking time out of his busy day to show around a foreign "sister" like me. In fact, he even insisted on making tea, which he served on a large, plastic table pulled into the middle of the garden.

As Luigi sat across from me, he waxed poetic about the place, its beauty and history. After that, there was the typical conversation— the standard diatribe against the Israeli occupation, the fact that he, as a Palestinian man, could not find satisfactory work, and the assertion that the Fathers at Bethesda treated him better than did his Muslim co-faithful.

So far, it was a typical script—until...

"I'm not happy with my wife."

Bloody hell...

"I feel comfortable talking to you..."

OK.... "Um...well, thank you, Majid. Um, it's time for me to be going now..." I said, rising from the table.

"But *sister*...I just feel like you understand me somehow. I mean, look, you talked to me and I didn't eat you."

Oh Lord...

"Well, yes, but it's getting late, and I have to go to another appointment...Thank you Majid...."

"Please take my number," he interrupted, scribbling the digits on a slip of paper. "Promise to call me. Please call me any time!" He paused, rethinking his plan. "Actually, don't call in the morning, though....only during the day..."

Sure thing, Luigi.

There was no doubt about it. So far, quite a few Muslim men had been very, well, friendly to me, and it was something I'd chalked up to the famous "Middle Eastern hospitality." At the same time, though, there seemed to often be an undercurrent of romantic interest that made me feel nervous and wary, mainly because I was completely unaccustomed to it back in the United States.

I had started wearing the *hijab*, or Islamic dress, when I was nineteen years old and in my first year of university. It consisted of a large, square scarf tied in a triangle like a babushka doll, and long trench-coat like garments called *jilbabs*. I certainly was not a hot co-ed on campus, and aside from a few adolescent crushes in middle school, I went straight from high school to marriage. All of this made me ill-prepared for the blatantly flirtatious nature of that seemed to afflict many Middle Eastern men...the interest, the subtle inquiry in the eyes, the turn of conversation, somehow and inevitably to the possibility that I just might be available (even though they knew I was married). It threw my confidence off balance, and it made me feel guilty, as if it was my fault somehow for being out and about alone—or that perhaps I was throwing off a weird vibe. It also pissed me off.

As I turned to walk away, again toward the Damascus Gate over the slippery cobblestones, I felt my body react to the experience with a weird surge of adrenaline that made my heart pound and my hands shake. It was literally the first time I'd been really hit on since I'd started wearing a *hijab*—and that was what—seventeen years ago. I was rattled…Call me, indeed!

But in truth, I was also a bit elated. After so many years of proper be-havior and decorum, which in essence consisted of the famous Muslim adage to "keep your eyes down," and expecting to always be "protected" by my husband, I would have imagined that some kind of disaster would befall me in a situation like that in Bethesda. After all, we practice strict segregation even at home, separating non-relative male "guests" and the "women of the house" like the majority of religious Muslim families we knew.

In my case, that meant it was normal for the women in my husband's family to often—for lack of a better word—*hide* in our own homes. When male guests were around, I would make the tea, arrange some cookies on plate, and then ring a specially designed bell for pick-up, signaling my husband or another relative to come and fetch it, lest I (gasp) appear before strange men.

I never really believed that this was the right, or even the Islamic, thing to do. In fact, it irked me and made me feel fake, subservient and used. It certainly didn't make sense in any way; after all, I went out all the time to the store, school, the bank, and other public places where men could see me. However, all the Arab women I knew in my circle and fam-ily acted the same way, and that was enough for me. If it was culturally expected, it became just another one of the things I did to fit in.

But like many things done for the wrong reason, it eventually caused a problem. And for me, following this custom resulted in my metamorphosis from a girl very good at affecting a fake-prissy propriety into someone with a real fear of the world. I was frightened to venture into the unknown, and developed an exaggerated fondness for well-beaten paths. Although I fit the part of a "good Arab wife," I didn't really believe in many of the behaviors that made me seem to be such. By visiting Bethesda alone and not asking "permission" from anyone first (or even telling anyone where I'd really be), or by visiting any other "non-essential" place, and especially by talking to "strange men," I was walking into the realm of unthinkable behavior, at least by Safa standards.

Although a part of me felt the prevailing wisdom against such wandering out was correct (sure enough, a guy had talked to me! He flirted! How could I put myself in such a situation!), it was also a revelation. Nothing else happened. For the first time I realized that years of exaggerated prudence had blurred the real lines of caution. I certainly wouldn't go overboard and tempt fate (and pepper spray would remain my trusty friend), but it was up to me to find my own limits.

It was then that I realized just what had resonated so much with me that day in my daughter's Taekwondo class. The truth was, I would have loved to join her, but when I thought about it, I knew my husband and most everyone else I then looked to for religious guidance would disapprove. After all, such action would involve contact with the (presumably, male) teacher, training with men, talking….certainly, it was improper. Amani was still young and the rules didn't apply (yet). So, although I bowed to propriety, I knew that she, too would soon be of age to bow—a thought that had filled me with a dread I could only now name. It was a lesson learned (one I could have only learned alone), and it was one fear I would never again allow to restrain either me or, I prayed, my daughter.

I took my leave of Luigi and his marital problems and walked out of the gate and started back up the Via Delarosa, leaving the cloud of fear and guilt behind me. Looking up, I could see that the Jerusalem sky was already tinged with the golden hue that signaled the turn into dusk, and the evening's coolness descended in the air. It was then that I realized that I could breathe more comfortably than I had in a long time.

Maybe there was something miraculous about Bethesda after all.

CHAPTER 17

Car Trouble

*It took me a long time not to judge myself
through someone else's eyes.*

-SALLY FIELD

My long afternoon in Jerusalem didn't go unnoticed. Although nobody really criticized me for it, I could sense that the family—especially my mother- and father-in-law—seemed to be unhappy with my mobility. I fully understood why. After all, my mobility was something that even the men in the family couldn't attain.

It was rare in for most families in Safa to own fully functioning cars, simply because they were so expensive. Instead, of those who owned cars at all, most of them preferred what was known as "*mashtoob*" or unregistered cars, due to the incredible expense and limited utility that registered cars bring.

Owning a car in the West Bank is frustrating. As a rule, cars are double-taxed by the Israeli government, in spite of the fact that Palestinian cars can't be driven inside Israeli territory or Jerusalem. They are limited within the West Bank to so-called "Arab" towns and roads (many of them nothing more than dirt tracks). Worst of all, though, is the fact that as a driver you can get ticketed by both Israeli police, who patrol the nice highways and watch the interchanges, and by the Palestinian Authority police who can only operate inside Palestinian towns. Add to that the facts that car prices are ridiculous, that gas is beyond expensive and that there really aren't many places left where Palestinian cars are allowed to go. They are prohibited from Jerusalem, any cities inside Israel proper (including all of the Palestinian villages inside the Green Line), Tel Aviv, Nazareth, any of the Mediterranean Sea, the Red Sea, or the Negev. This left Palestinian drivers with the big four West Bank cities of Hebron, Bethlehem, Ramallah and Nablus (although it used to be possible for West Bank Palestinians to visit Jericho and the Dead Sea, recently access has been increasingly denied by roving checkpoints that turn back Palestinians from visiting this last body of water, too).

Given all of this, most villagers, my husband's family included, used *mashtoob* cars, which could be had for a fraction of the cost, usually because they were stolen by middle-men (Jewish and Palestinian) from inside Israel. Thus, *mashtoob* cars were unlicensed and uninsurable, they could only be driven safely inside the village (as the Israeli and Palestinian police rarely entered small villages like Safa), and were basically only good for grocery shopping and local transport.

Now, if I was unique in my mobility compared to the family men, I was positively alien compared to the women, so I should have expected a bit of an adjustment as they realized this. Although I tried to fit as much as I could into the domestic lives of the women around me, there was no ignoring the fact that I would be different than the average village wife, who might literally spend the majority of her life at home.

I could work where I wanted, buy the groceries I liked, pay my electricity or phone bill, go shopping, and even sneak around visiting all of the random places my heart desired. Yes, for the most part, I could avoid or somehow circumvent the restrictions most Palestinians were forced to deal with, whether male or female. Surely that aroused some envy. And even if my father- or brothers-in-law or students didn't begrudge me the priceless mobility my passport bought me, it wasn't as easy to shake off the feeling that I was somehow doing something wrong.

Like a tiny rock stuck in your sandal, my car became a symbol of everything that made me objectionable and foreign, and at first I didn't quite realize that every time I ventured out of Safa with or without the kids, I was pushing the limits of acceptable behavior. Although I knew it wasn't typical for women to come and go as they pleased, I somehow imagined myself exempt from the rules. Only it wasn't that easy—a fact I soon realized as I read an email from my husband, Ahmad, in Seattle, chiding me for "running around" the country—although we'd previously agreed that I would be looking for something about my experience in the Holy Land to write about (a task that might be a bit difficult without actually "running around").

Although he did cool down after I reminded him of this fact, I still felt the sting of his words—and a lurking apprehension about the way the family was obviously "reporting" the things they didn't like about me behind my back, Still, I defended myself as much as I could in an email, and things seemed to smooth over until I made my next "transgression," the fallout from what I considered to be one of the most beautiful nights of my life.

The Old City at night is breathtaking: its walls all floodlit and glowing up to heaven, the golden Dome of the Rock's roof is illuminated, bright and dazzling against the starry sky. But that's just the view from the outside. Inside the city walls, the crowds have disappeared, and gone are the noises of the market; the blaring Arabic pop songs, belching tractors, and honking horns all die down and you are left with an almost complete silence that suits the place. It's really the best way to pretend—if for a few moments here and there—that you are walking the streets of ancient Jerusalem.

The city probably looked much the same at night as it has for centuries: dark, empty alleyways, shuttered shop doors, and trash-strewn streets resembling the grounds of a state fair just after closing. The feeling I had, though, was one of pure exhilaration, as if I were doing something incredibly daring just being there—a fact reinforced by virtually every guidebook on the market, official and unofficial; all warning against the perils of being stuck in the dark alleyways of the Old City at night. Unfortunately, the Old City probably *was* dangerous at night; especially if you happened to be hanging around the "wrong place."

That meant it wasn't a good idea to be an Palestinian dawdling in the Jewish Quarter, nor was it advisable for a Jew to hang out in the Muslim, Christian, or Armenian Quarters (although the Armenians generally closed their gates to outsiders at night). As long as you knew the lay of the city enough to know who "owned" the neighborhood, the risk of anything untoward happening to you was relatively low. More, if you were a local-looking mom with her kids along in the Old City, it led to a sense of respectability that virtually guaranteed protection from attempts at sexual harassment or other danger.

As for the kids and me, we found it heavenly, particularly the night that we discovered the Temple Mount in all of its glory; the crowds were gone, and just the sound of the wind whistling through the palm, olive, and pine trees remained. There the Dome shined like a jewel under the soft indigo sky, and I sat talking to Bushra—a friend from America who had recently relocated back to Jerusalem—while our kids played hide and seek in the giant courtyard next to the fountain, spraying up into the air, adding to the soundtrack of the place. The kids loved it, and as I sat chatting with my friend I felt relaxed and at peace. Yes, I felt very lucky to be in this beautiful place.

The drive home was another matter altogether. I'd been warned against driving at night in the West Bank with my yellow plates. During the day the kids and I were readily identifiable by my headscarf and *hatta* (the hallmark black and white scarf that is the unofficial symbol of the Palestinian people) which I'd draped over my dashboard, lest we in any way resemble a car full of Israeli settlers. But at night it was a crap-shoot—we could be anyone.

That meant I not only had to get us through the checkpoints success-fully, I also had to worry about attacks that I'd heard happen to people driving along the roads—especially at night. I was new enough in the country not to know the actual degree of danger we could be in. Did the attacks happen every day? Every month? Every few months? Once again, there was no reliable guide to who or what was actually dangerous, and the more time passed, the more I realized that the ability to live with uncertainty was an integral characteristic of life here in the Holy Land. It was a skill I would have to develop, and fast. It was with this in mind that I first pondered the question of the sunroof.

My favorite part of my Volkswagen Polo, other than its yellow plates, was the retractable roof. Not quite as open as a convertible but more so than a regular sunroof, the entire top of the car opened up like an accor-dion in a way I hadn't seen on any cars back in the United States.

I loved it normally, but on the highway out of Jerusalem I felt a little differently. As a beautiful four-lane, well-lit highway, snaking through the heart of the West Bank, it was a source of irritation: signaling the triumph of the settler movement, the vast developmental gap between the occupiers and the occupied (who couldn't take advantage of the nice, shiny stretch). But once you passed the huge settlement blocs just south of Jerusalem, it narrowed and funneled into a dark, winding, pitch black, back-country road, marked with giant, tire-popping pot holes. It also held the specter of lurking, pissed-off Palestinian teenagers with pockets full of stones. This was the "Arab section" of the roadway, serving the major cities of Bethlehem, Hebron, and the countless smaller towns and villages south of Jerusalem.

Because this was my first night drive outside of the village, I was scared as hell and grew increasingly nervous as I drove on toward the village and into the darkest, most winding part of the road. During the day, my scarf made it clear that I wasn't an Israeli settler, but at night it would be easy to be mistaken for a tasty target. Many Israelis—some entire families, in fact— had been stoned here, shot at, or even ambushed and killed, and I suddenly had an awful vision of the car engulfed in flames with the kids inside. I closed the roof.

It was actually the cause of an old practical debate, this potential projectile problem. Sure, having the roof closed was obvious; I'd rather have a Molotov bounce off it than land inside. But the windows—that was where the debate came in.

Which was worse? A rock flying inside an open window might miss its target, but a good hit to a window would mean adding thousands of tiny pieces of glass to the mix. I always let the kids keep their windows open, and by the time I neared the Aroub Palestinian refugee camp, a warren of ugly cement homes built up on top of one another, it seemed especially dark and foreboding behind the giant chain-length fence (installed by the Israeli Army in an attempt to quell the rock throwing from the residents).

I was at my wits end as, eyes wide, trying to scan the sides of the road for any threats, I readied myself for the last stretch of road to the village. And that's when Amani announced she had to go to the bathroom, *immediately*!

I won't lie. I contemplated letting her pee in her pants. That's how frightened I was by the stories everyone had told me about the highway. Instead, I pulled over and lifted her over the guardrail so she could quickly go, but by the time we reached the looming guard tower at the turnoff toward the village, I was giddy with relief. Little did I know that the dramatic events of the night were just getting started.

I drove through the fog that usually descended on Safa after dark; it was misty, dense, and blown across the buildings, streets, and fields in the village in large clouds. As I neared home, all of the neighboring houses—including that of my mother-in-law, were dark. *Great*, I thought, relieved. *I don't have to talk to anyone until tomorrow.*

I pulled the car into the garage, exhausted but happy that the day had turned out just fine. I'd just put Karim to bed and set about changing into my pajamas when I heard it. Bang! Bang! Bang! Someone was pounding their fists on the steel garage doors. *What the…*It was far past midnight, and, afraid the noise would wake up Karim, I quickly finished dressing while hurrying to the garage to open the door.

"Jenny!" *Iftahi al bab!* "Open the door!" I pushed the button and opened the garage doors, their loud motors rolling up before the figures of my mother- and father-in-law, standing outside in the cold wind.

As soon as the door was high enough to pass under, they both rushed in, obviously angry that I was so late, but maybe a little unsure of how to deal with me and my "transgression." Unable to yell at me properly (I feigned incomprehension), they resorted to camping out on the couches, obviously intending to spend the night in my living room where they could keep a closer eye on me, a woman out of control.

Frustrated and tired, I nevertheless pretended to be oblivious to their anger. Still, I thoroughly enjoyed the way my usual nightly swarm of mosquitoes attacked them and their fresh blood while they slept, and I smiled in satisfaction as I watched them cover their heads with blankets in an attempt to shield themselves from the onslaught. Soon, though, we were all asleep; them in the living room, and me and the kids in the master bedroom. There I piled what must have been a half-foot of blankets on top of us to keep warm (and where I had a nice, new plug-in mosquito repellent).

When I awoke the next morning, I readied myself for some kind of lecture, but when I came out of the room, all dressed, coifed and made up in my armor, I was surprised to see them gone. Suddenly I felt guilty. Maybe they were just relieved that I got home safely. Maybe they weren't mad at all. *Yes*, I thought. It was possible that I'd misunderstood. Perhaps they'd decided they might as well sleep over rather than take the long walk across the street back to their house.

Yeah, right.

As it turned out, what my dear in-laws really did was hurry home at the first hint of dawn, call Ahmad in America, and report my irresponsible and scandalous behavior, *tout de suite*.

Judging from his reaction, they did a bang-up job.

CHAPTER 18

Sister Wives

Contempt is the weapon of the weak and a defense against one's own despised and unwanted feelings.

-ALICE MILLER

The following day, I received a nasty email from America in which Ahmad demanded I start acting like a "good, Muslim woman," presumably more like my sisters-in-law. What they had told him I wasn't exactly sure, but from his "good woman" remark I realized that his anger wasn't aimed at the possible dangers we could have faced on the road or even in the city at night.

Clearly the real issue was my desire to go anywhere according to my whim. It was completely alien to the family, something that had never happened before. Although I could understand the discomfort that my relative independence caused, it was still frustrating to be forced to battle their nebulous belief that a "good woman" stays home, or if she did go out—especially at night—she always went under the "protection" of a man.

Now, it wasn't that I didn't understand the cultural forces at work. I knew very well that this was the dominant attitude of many Muslims before I'd arrived in Jerusalem. What did surprise me, though, was the venom in the criticism, the implication that I'd done something not just unwise, but shameful. After all, Ahmad had regularly "allowed" me to go out alone at night in America (where nobody in Safa would know about it), yet he seemed to think nothing of insulting me for my forays over here. And he hadn't bothered to ask me about my side of the story. It was enough that his parents didn't like it.

Still, as I sat there at the kitchen table, staring in shock at the email, I realized that for once I was as angry with the criticism as I was hurt—no small change, considering how sensitive I was to any criticism from him when I'd been back in America, and even how much the previous "running around" email succeeded in wounding my feelings.

I knew for sure that I was going to continue our excursions out of the village. If I didn't, I would not only have virtually nothing to write about, but I would be bored out of my mind. And then there was the thought of falling in line with the "ideal Safa womanhood" bullshit (much in the way I'd embraced some of the other cultural practices I didn't agree with over the years). The very thought got under my skin.

Still, I had to be practical. After all, I'd scarcely been here six months, and I certainly didn't want to alienate everyone in the family, so for a while I tried to employ a bit more subtlety, making a special point of being home before sunset.

I strongly resented the pressure to conform to Safa standards of ideal womanhood and the huge difference between being an Arab and being a Muslim. After all, the world's Asian/Pacific Muslim population far exceeds the Middle Eastern one. The thousands of other cultures around the world that call themselves "Muslim," from China to Bosnia to Sub-Saharan Africa, each have their own cultural quirks that are quite separate from Islam as a faith. I was a Muslim and had no problem being judged on the basis of my religion (which I chose and willfully embraced).

However, I would not willingly take on the cultural expectations the family had for me as a woman. I knew I wasn't doing anything "wrong," but it was still frustrating. I'd expected Safa to be at least on some levels a "haven of belonging" that I hadn't found in America, but it wasn't, and the thought that there might not be such a "place" for me anywhere began to intrude more and more into my carefully maintained view of the world.

For all of my growing internal bravado, though, I was becoming lonely. Lonelier, even, than I had been in Seattle—where I'd been plenty lonely. It wasn't fun being the only Muslim mom on the local PTA, or at the neighborhood BYOB block party. That was bad enough. But now I was in an unfamiliar place and under the pressure of so many major changes: being alone, working, trying to manage the house, the kids, the language…I was terrified that the loneliness might transform into a too-familiar dark shadow of depression and anxiety, and I knew that I could not afford to "lose it" here.

In desperation, I fell back on my oldest and most dysfunctional coping mechanism: trying to please as many people as possible. Like a woman possessed, I worked my ass off, ferrying family members to the doctor, bringing them groceries, letting them borrow my car—even though it was illegal and could get me arrested. I did everything I could to score points and fit in.

Still, it seemed that no matter what I did, someone wanted more. There were so many of them, and each seemed to think they—and only they—deserved a piece of me, complaining when I took this one to the doctor or another one to the store in town. It actually seemed that my strategy was beginning to backfire.

It all finally came to a head one night on a trip to the local grocery. Up until then, my usual routine would be a general announcement that I was going to the store and if anyone wanted to come, *ahlanwasahlan*, "Welcome."

"If you can fit, you can come," was my motto. Usually this meant puttering the short distance to the "supermarket" hole-in-the-wall, the car stuffed with kids on a candy mission, blasting music and laughter into the low Judean hills.

The kids and their cousins loved these outings, and the competition to be one of the chosen few to go sometimes led to meltdowns. I tried to be as fair as I could, rotating turns between the seemingly endless supply of cousins. One night, though, the lot of them tested my patience, instigating a "who gets to ride with Auntie Jenny" kid brawl after I'd managed to wedge at least twelve of them into the Polo like a clown car.

Furious, I stopped the car in front of Huda's house and ordered all of them, including my own, out of the car. There was nothing too strange about that, especially given that many of the other parents in Safa beat their kids. I was mad, but I hoped they would learn that their candy runs were not guaranteed benefits from the American aunt.

That's why I was so shocked when my mother-in-law asked me the next day why I called the kids "Arab Dogs"—one of the worst insults in the Arabic language—during the melee. Now, I do have a temper, and I was known for hurling f-bombs back in America at the occasional racist or homicidal lane-changer. But I do have some scruples when it comes to nasty insults: I save them for the grown-ups. What my mother-in-law repeated to me was an outright lie.

I was so mad that I demanded to know the source of the accusation, thinking perhaps it was one of the kids out of his mind from sugar withdrawal. When she told me instead that Asya and Sa'eda were the sources of the information, I felt a white-hot anger flash through me.

I wanted to wring their necks! Although a part of me wasn't surprised that Asya had come up with such a thing, I really couldn't understand Sa'eda's involvement. *They picked on the wrong princess this time,*

damn it. There was no way I was going to let it go. In fact, I was so upset that I took it to the extreme and brought in every witness I could find, including all the kids, parading them into my in-laws' kitchen where they all gathered to hear me rant in my (surprisingly improved) Arabic.

"You're a liar, Asya, and you know it." I yelled. "I'm going to call Ahmad, and I'm going to make you swear to God that I said it." Asking a religious (or even a quasi-religious) Muslim swear to God about anything is a dire thing, and they take it very seriously. "Swear it, Asya."

Asya's face froze ever so slightly while she thought it over, presumably considering the otherworldly consequences of sticking to her story. "Maybe I didn't hear you right…" she started.

At that, I fixed her and Sa'eda (who sat cowed and mute the entire time) with the ugliest glare I could muster, turned and went home vindicated—sort of.

I should have felt better, but despite my victory, I couldn't shake the feeling that everyone had been pretty darn quick to believe them against me. I'd been in Safa for months now, but I was still the "outsider," a piece of sand in the shorts of the homogeneous village. I began to realize that no matter how hard I tried, or how many times I ferried my sister-in-laws' kids to the store, took people to the doctor or dentist, tried to look like a Palestinian, dress like one, act like one, marry one…or give birth to three children…I would never be one of them. Not really.

Sure, I felt sorry for myself, although I should have understood that I was a big change for them all, a real shake-up for them and for their lives, and I couldn't really blame Asya for being a bit of a snappy puppy. During other circumstances I might have given her, or them, a pass. But alone, tired, and trying to navigate this new life myself, I wasn't prepared to be Madame Understanding. I was prepared to mope, kvetch and court the paranoia that was probably inevitable. Unfortunately, this was exactly when my father-in-law stopped coming over to supervise the still-ongoing construction outside or my during kids' bi-weekly Arabic lesson (taught by a man in my living room at night, no less)!

I took it as a clear signal that my husband and his family didn't care about me—after all, custom said that the entire family's honor was threatened by leaving me alone with the workers, to say nothing of the tutor. It simply wasn't done—ever. So, instead of thinking of any of the other possible reasons for my father-in-law's lapse of duty (like, perhaps, his fondness for long afternoon naps), I seethed in a stew of resentment until I finally decided to stop telling him when I left the village, a respectful gesture I'd been careful to make until then.

It only took a few days of this before my father-in-law called Ahmad again to complain about me, only this time he suggested Ahmad should possibly marry another wife. In Islam and in Palestine, a man can marry up to four wives, but the practice is generally uncommon, especially among the younger generation. Although I'd been a Muslim for more than a decade, I'd never met a polygamous couple in Safa or the United States. It was so unusual, in fact, that almost everyone in the family was shocked when Khalid married his brother's widow—but that was how it turned out.

The day Jamal died was like any other, they said. Married three months before, Jamal was serious about making as much money as he could scrape together to support his new wife. So when he went out that morning to go antique hunting in the hills outside of Jerusalem, nobody thought to say any special goodbyes. The next time they saw him, he was gone: killed almost instantly when his car rolled over just north of the city. His son was born six months later.

It was then, and at my father-in-law's insistence (at one point, he smashed out all of Khalid and Asya's front windows and drove them out of their house), that Khalid "stepped up" and married Sawsan to keep her and the baby in Safa, instead of going back to her family in a distant village as custom otherwise demanded. To add insult to injury, however, Asya found out just like everybody else the afternoon Khalid returned from signing the marriage contract, Sawsan in tow.

Still, there was nothing she could do. Asya had six kids, no job, no education, and a family that thought it better if she just swallowed her pride and accepted her fate. Maybe they thought she'd get used to it. She didn't. It was more than a decade later, and Asya was just as bitter about the marriage as she was that first day—she just got better at managing the bile.

Like most people in the family, I didn't hide the fact that I thought the idea of Khalid marrying Sawsan was a mistake. But, as people like my father-in-law hastened to point out, polygamy is a part of Islam. Still, I guess I just saw it from a different point of view.

Polygamy *is* allowed in Islam (but is not legal in several Muslim countries), and although many non-Muslims know about the practice, few understand its place in the religion. Unlike the fundamentalist Mormon sects we hear so much about in the United States, plural marriage is not considered a path to heaven; in fact, it's not even recommended in the Quran, which states, "...marry women of your choice, two or three or four; but if you fear that you shall not be able to deal justly with them, then only one."

Of course, many polygamous men preferred to "forget" the tail end of the verse, and it showed. After all, it would take a rare bird to be completely fair to more than one spouse or lover at a time, and Khalid—nice as he was—wasn't that kind of bird. In fact, considering all of the tears, fighting, and hurt feelings I'd seen between the three of them (not to mention the kids) in the barely half-year I'd been on the scene, the only real result of their union was two broken homes instead of one.

As for the wives, they were about as far from the "sister wife" ideal as you could get; although they could put on a terrific show for outsiders. It was odd, but I suppose they just got tired of staying in a state of constant turmoil, so they sat together at night outside my mother-in-law's house, worked together if the occasion demanded it, even laughed together sometimes. But separate them and place one before a sympathetic ear, and the rage fairly poured out of them—Asya, because her husband of twenty years, and presumably the love of her life, had married Sawsan. Sawsan, for her part, knew damn well that she had been taken on out of duty. Both women felt humiliated in their own way, and I felt the whole situation was pretty much unsatisfactory to everyone involved. That, and to be honest, it simply grossed me out.

Such was my mindset when I heard that my father-in-law was encouraging my husband to marry another wife. I'd overheard this little tidbit from my mother-in-law as she chatted with two of Ahmad's aunts about him over cups of thick, Arabic coffee. I'd been rounding the corner with a cup of my own when I heard her say, "Abu Ahmad (Ahmad's father) said he should marry a girl from here…"

I froze. In fact, at first I wasn't sure if I'd heard her right, and I waited a few seconds for my brain to translate and re-translate the words, standing like an idiot with my coffee cup in my hand.

I had no idea if she'd simply forgotten that I was within hearing distance, assumed I couldn't understand, or perhaps wanted me to overhear. But by the time I'd processed the comment enough for my face –and mood—to darken, I knew that she knew she'd made a terrible mistake.

"Did you say that Abu-Ahmad told Ahmad to get married?" I asked.

"No..no..sweetie," she answered, "We just want you to have another baby…Just one more son…"

How I hated them!

Although I knew Ahmad wouldn't do such a thing, or expect me to stand for it, I was so hurt, depressed, and frustrated that I holed up in the house with the kids for weeks. When I wasn't at work I was at home, maniacally painting *trompe l'oeil* murals on the bare cement walls and crying myself to sleep at night. I refused to see anyone.

It wasn't even that I believed they were serious about Ahmad re-marrying. In fact, I suspected it was a kind of passive-aggressive "shot across the bow" to get my attention, up the ante, and show me who was boss. Still, even when Ahmad tried to calm me down on the phone when I brought up the subject, joking about it while at the same time urging me to try and "fix things" between myself and the family, there was no way I was going to budge. I wasn't going to be "the bigger person." Instead, I made up my mind that I was going to stay on my own, completely separated from them. I was convinced as only someone isolated in a new family, community, culture and language can be convinced, that I was an abject object of hate, envy, scorn and annoyance. I was just too hurt and insecure to re-engage, so I became more isolated and angry, wallowing in self-pity.

I worked, took the kids places, and spent hours alone on a hidden balcony high on the house, drinking my Starbucks stash and watching the clouds and their shadows moving over the hills and valleys on their way from the Mediterranean sea. I also spied on my wicked sisters-in-law during their nightly strolls on the road in front of my house, straining to hear the subject of their conversation, and convinced it was me.

I knew it was pitiful for a thirty-six year-old woman to hide in the shadows watching the "in" crowd go by. But as determined as I was to show them all that I didn't need them anyway, I was also scared, lonely, and hurt. I was just too stubborn to let it show or to pack it in and leave for home, which I probably would have done eventually if a falafel sandwich hadn't changed everything.

CHAPTER 19

A Safa Thanksgiving

Forgiveness is the answer to the child's dream of a miracle
by which what is broken is made whole again, what is soiled
is made clean again.

- DAG HAMMARSKJOLD

I may have *thought* I could handle life in the village without being a part of the family, but my stomach quickly brought home the true meaning of hubris. It was early evening and I was coming home from work on the Jerusalem highway, my stomach rumbling louder than Pink's *Funhouse* (which had become my anthem during the previous weeks). In fact, I'd been wallowing in a self-pity that grew with each passing day, and I'd developed a soundtrack to go with it. But as I drove I was slowly becoming aware that things might get worse for me. What I didn't know was the time was fast approaching.

It wasn't the first time I'd been sick in Palestine. On my previous visit, about three years before, I'd been afflicted with what seemed to me one of the plagues of Job—thousands of tiny canker sores covering the inside of my mouth. It was horrible, but at least then, Ahmad had been there to help—to interpret, watch the kids and hold my hand (as I medicated myself out of the experience with whatever opioids Dr. Muhammad could give to me).

This time I walked in the house as darkness was falling, dropped my laptop bag on the floor, and lay down on the couch, riding out the first real wave of pain and dread I was to become intimately acquainted with that night. I was alone, the kids needed dinner, and I was growing sicker by the minute—pretty sure I'd fallen prey to food poisoning.

Hoping to ride it out, I hurried to make the kids what had become their favorite fast food: fresh Arabic *Taboon* bread topped with green olive oil, garlic and the local Israeli pasteurized process cheese food that passed acceptably for mozzarella. I broiled it all to a bubbly crisp under my oven's gigantic gas burner while I stood there holding my stomach, praying that the pain wouldn't get any worse.

However, by the time the kids were finished eating and cozy in their beds, I was huddled on the couch with cramps so knife-sharp they reminded me of labor pains. Still, it was only when I started vomiting as well, and realized I would probably have to stay in the bathroom all night, that I started to panic. I was convinced I'd fallen prey to a fatal case of *something*, probably contracted from one of downtown Hebron's falafel stands that my students had repeatedly (and ineffectively) warned me about.

An hour went by, then two. By midnight I was trying hard not to scream from the pain, and my moaning had scared Ibrahim enough to go and get Manar for help, despite my protests. By the time she and Huda returned a few minutes later, I could barely talk, reduced to huddling miserably on the bed and crying pitifully. Whatever bug had me, it was taking its job seriously—so seriously, in fact, that when my mother-in-law arrived, the first thing I did was look up at her with my mascara-streaked face and ask her to please, "Help me die."

I didn't even try to maintain the careful facade I usually presented around Ahmad's, family. When you're really sick, you're also really, really *human*. Your ego is one of the first things to go.

In Palestine there seemed to be a general preference for my type of appearance: pale skin, blonde hair, blue or green eyes, and a round face (the bane of my existence back home). Consequently, I could hardly be blamed for my pride in my appearance. It seemed to be my claim to fame, especially because culturally, linguistically, and socially I often felt like a bumbling idiot.

So when my breathlessly beautiful looks were gone, as they must be whilst puking one's guts out to an audience, I was surprised that it just didn't bother me. There was no pretense of perfection, no toughing it out and no stiff upper lip. I was a sobbing, retching, wild-haired mess, and I needed their help. As more people arrived, the pain grew to terrible, wringing cramps in my gut that made me tremble and cry between the bouts of nausea. Whenever I closed my eyes, visions of e-coli bacteria, squirming in their microscopic horrid evilness, swirled in my head. I knew that I was becoming dehydrated and probably needed an IV, but the thought of repeating Karim's experience in that Bethlehem hospital only made me feel worse.

As for Jerusalem's modern hospitals, I hadn't counted on the fact that maybe I would be the next one to need them. I was certainly in no condition to drive myself anywhere, and as nobody in the family had a permit to cross the checkpoint, I decided that I wasn't budging from home.

Word quickly spread in Safa that I was sick, and family members—at first, all women—began to pour into the house until at least forty people were standing around me, wringing their hands and offering clucking encouragement as I lay in the middle of the living room floor on one of the foam mattresses—bucket at the ready.

By the time Sameeha showed up at the scene with her daughter, the room was packed with women and kids standing around my mattress in a semicircle. Parting the crowd with her usual assurance, she took one look at me and pulled out her cell phone to summon Dr. Muhammad, which prompted a flurry of activity as the women searched for a scarf to cover my hair. It was a move that, for some reason, sparked a flash of anger in me. I remember I even tried to push the blasted thing away when they put it over my head.

Who the hell would look at my hair right now?! I thought. It just hit me as fundamentally stupid. Still, I was in no condition to make any philosophical arguments, so I let them finish pinning it on before the doctor arrived.

Of course, it turned out that the women were right. The arrival of the doctor meant that I was properly covered, which the men of the family took it as a green light to follow in his wake so they, too, could take a gander at me—just to make sure my last shred of dignity be properly extinguished. Stepping in through the parting crowd, he knelt next to the mattress with his characteristic calm and asked, "So what seems to be the problem?"

If by then Arabic was gone from my linguistic capabilities, what with all of my energy going toward things like puking and crying, I still managed to make my insistence that I would not to go to the hospital for rehydration very clear in simple, if flowery English—and a short, choppy diatribe about how I wasn't going to die in one of those "filthy places."

Understanding as ever, the doctor walked home to fetch an IV and a strong shot for the pain, with which he quickly returned to administer in front of the crowd. It was at that moment—with a rivulet of blood rolling down my arm, and the delicious rush of relief flooding my body, that I swore he was the best doctor on the fucking planet.

It wasn't until the next day when I woke up that I learned the rest of what happened that night, particularly how I'd fallen asleep in front of the whole family while they took turns holding the IV bag aloft for five minutes at a time—for three hours. And suddenly, I loved these people.

Well, most of them.

My Arabic kept on improving in spite my lack of real study, but that's probably because I'd settled for atrocious grammar and single-form verbs. Still, in spite of sounding like a precocious toddler, I noticed that lately I began feeling as if I could really communicate and—perhaps more important—understand what was being said. I was actually starting to find conversation, particularly Safa gossip, fascinating. I enjoyed that constant running hum of commentary, interpretation, invention and re-invention of the story of the village and its people!

I couldn't deny that I felt much closer to the family after I recovered from my stomach bug, and I even started participating in communal chores, including scything wheat that grew wild on the hillsides that would later be roasted into the smoky kernels that were added to a meat soup called *Freekah*. This was an activity Asya and most of the other younger women disdained, but I loved it—rather like the days I spent as a teenager mucking out the cow stalls at the county fair.

It was even more peaceful to work alongside my mother and father-in-law, the family horse, and the flock of sheep brought along to graze. I didn't even mind when the large turtle I found under the stalks (thankfully before I made my slash with the scythe) saw fit to shit directly onto my open-toed sandals as I held it aloft in pride. It hadn't even occurred to me that they *did* that!

There was no doubt about it; I was developing a thing for the village's pastoral pastimes—carrying water, picking shiny new grape leaves to make delicious *Warag Dawali* (leaves rolled like cigars filled with rice, garlic, tomatoes, lemon and cooked atop layers of chicken, onions and more garlic—tons of it in a huge pot a-simmer—good Lord, it's heaven), cooking the large communal *Mansafs* in cauldrons over giant propane burners, trying to make bread like Huda.

This was, in fact, the one aspect of village life that seemed to be acting as a balm to what had become over the years a real tendency toward deep and unrelenting depression. For me, it was a "Chop Wood, Carry Water" realization.

Of course, a part of me knew that most of the charm of these *Little House on the Prairie* moments probably corresponded to their novelty. After all, I certainly didn't see any locals rushing to the fields if they didn't have to, but I decided to go with it anyway. Years of therapy, medication, and self-help books had failed to address the chronic melancholy that plagued me, so I wasn't going to ignore the fact that my spirits were lifting when I did my field work. I'd take what I could get.

Taking the sheep out to pasture, learning to tie and stack sheaves of wheat like days of yore, and figuring out how to clean turtle crap from between my toes with wadded chaff felt good.

And that's when the turkeys came.

Turkeys are not native to the Holy Land, and it wasn't until Israeli poultry farmers brought large-scale turkey farms to the region that their meat began to be consumed occasionally; which probably explained why most of the Palestinians I knew had no real idea how to cook it whole. It just wasn't deep enough in their food history yet.

So when Khalid brought in a surprise buy of about two hundred turkeys to sell and slaughter, I decided to buy and cook one of them in the traditional American style—after all, I had a couple of generations of North American turkey knowhow in my genes (and if necessary, I could call my grandma back in Oregon for her recipes). We would have a full Thanksgiving dinner—I'm sure for the first time in Safa history.

It wasn't until I'd helped the other wives clean and skin their turkeys that I knew I'd bitten off more than I could chew. These were no Butterballs, all clean and ready to stuff. No, these were walking, pooping, giant, frickin' strong birds, covered in feathers, full of life, that made eye-contact, for Pete's sake!

Still, I'd said I wanted one....and everyone who was anyone in Safa was getting one, so I waited my turn, chose the nearest turkey in view and in so doing marked him for death. One muttered *Bismillah* ("In the name of Allah," a phrase uttered at every animal slaughter), and there I had it—a giant dead, feathered, bloating bird. And then I realized my mistake.

It was huge, ridiculously huge! I must have grossly miscalculated when I'd sized up the live animal, but with all of the others around, it didn't look that big. It was only after I had it finally gutted (a disgusting procedure that I have no wish to repeat—ever) that I realized how heavy it was—certainly over fifty pounds—and I still had to pluck the sucker in the bathtub with pots of scalding water. It took two of us to lift it out.

After finding a large piece of sheet metal to cook the bird on, I set about finding the ingredients I needed to cook the meal, and the next day, after waking up at three in the morning to start the roasting, I prepared huge quantities of mashed potatoes, gravy, stuffing, dinner rolls, and my grandmother's delicious escalloped corn. Every dish was made from scratch.

By afternoon, the house was full of the same people who'd held up my IV bag when I was convinced they all hated me, all of them eating my exotic fare with flimsy plastic spoons and plates on long plastic sheets I'd spread on the floor. The only thing missing was pumpkin pie and cranberries. Still, it was the best Thanksgiving I'd had in ages.

CHAPTER 20

Shifting Normal

It is possible to be different and still be all right.

-Anne Wilson Schaef

Peter Shaneb looked just like a vampire—or at least what I imagined one would look like before *Twilight* ruined my mental picture. Tall, dark, with a widow's peak and a long salt and pepper ponytail, he was founding a fledgling Christian organization in Jerusalem called The Holy Landers, a name evoking images of medieval knights on crusade.

I met Peter after reading a posting on a Jerusalem Christian message board about lesser- known miraculous Christian sites in the area. As I sat across from him at a little bistro table on the balcony of the old Jerusalem Imperial Hotel, I couldn't help but notice that he looked resigned, somehow, as if he'd realized only too late that "they" had won. According to Peter, infighting, personal interests, and the financial, emotional, and physical stress of life under military occupation had sapped the community of its critical mass. Slowly but surely, the Palestinian Christian community was dying out.

The total number of Palestinian Christians remaining in the Holy Land is estimated to represent between 40,000 and 90,000 people in the West Bank and Gaza, with a further 144,000 to 200,000 inside of Israel.

Descendants of the first Christians, the once-robust Palestinian Christian community has dwindled to endangered status, with the majority living abroad. Still, despite the relatively low percentage of Palestinians who are Christian (about one in seventy-five), Peter still found it astonishing that relatively few Western Christians seemed to know about their community at all. Even worse, some (including the same tourists who aimed their cameras down from their giant tour busses, slumming for a few hours in Bethlehem) considered this group of Christians irrelevant, a bump on the road of a prophecy that said that the future of the world and the Second Coming of Jesus depended upon the triumph of Israel.

The question of whether the descendants of the first Christian disciples deserved to survive in the Holy Land seemed far less important than the success of the Jewish State, and that was an idea that indigenous Christians like Peter felt they could not embrace for obvious reasons.

It was Peter, struggling to start his own Christian organization, actually, more of a kind of social club, aimed at convincing the younger generation to stay around the country, who told me that if I was looking for an interesting, creepy, miraculous Christian story, I should check with another, larger organization in Jerusalem called *Sabeel*.

That's when I heard about the dead body.

Omar Haramy, a young Palestinian Christian, welcomed me into his office at Sabeel's Jerusalem headquarters. This organization was co-founded by Palestinian Christians and endorsed by Desmond Tutu to challenge the idea that Palestinians (Muslim and Christian) were doomed to continue this occupation according to the "will of God." It also supported continued non-violent resistance to the Israeli occupation.

Sabeel was a growing organization, with chapters in eleven Western countries, including the United States. Its goal was to support the local

Christian community, educate the world about the plight of the Palestinian people and, according to Omar, "get in the way" of the occupation.

Obviously used to visitors of a more political bent, Omar nonetheless was happy to give me some suggestions about some of the more unusual Christian sites around the country. Ticking off the obvious places,
his eyes suddenly lit up. "Well, there's the monastery in Al Lud, where St.
George was tortured to death. They still have the chains, which they say
are miraculous!" Then, he said, much like an afterthought, "Of course,
there's the miracle of the murdered priest up in Nablus..."

"What was that all about?" I interrupted, leaning forward in my chair.

"There was this priest who was a caretaker up at Jacob's Well in
Nablus. Well, there were some settlers there who got mad because they
wanted the site, so they killed him with an ax. Anyway, the cool thing is
that his body is still there, looking the same as the day he died."

"And when did he die, Omar?" I asked.

"Oh, I think something like thirty years ago," he replied with a grin.

Nablus is located in the northern West Bank. It's one of the cities in
the Holy Land outside of Jerusalem and Bethlehem that still has a size-
able Christian population, as well as being the only surviving community of Samaritans. It has tons of history and an ancient vaulted market that
rivals Jerusalem's. It was also reported to have the best *Kanefe*—a baked
confection consisting of a layer of sweet, locally produced cheese, but-
tery dough, and hot, sugary syrup—in the entire region. I decided to go,
regardless of the fact that this was probably going to be a frivolous jaunt.

For some women, I think many, little decisions are never made because it is just too much trouble to explain the urge to do them. One
of the great things about being in Palestine, though—maybe the best
thing—was the fact that I could choose to go wherever I wanted without

explaining myself to anyone, and if I really had to, it was usually only after I returned, *fait accompli*. Surprisingly, though, it seemed that now that the family and I really started to know each other, I began to look forward to telling them about my plans—because they seemed to actually be starting to get me.

Before visiting Nablus, though, was the first time that I really told the family in advance where I was going: Why, to see a dead body in a church, of course! And this time they didn't bat an eyelash. Although it probably didn't hurt that I promised to bring them back some Nablus *Kanefe*…

The road to Nablus from Jerusalem is hilly and marked by sweeping green pastures and winding roads. Unfortunately, it also had one of the most notorious and volatile checkpoints in Palestine just outside of the city of Huwwara.

Because it was one of the larger checkpoints, located in an area dotted with Israeli settlements and patrols, I knew that getting through probably wouldn't be an easy or pleasant experience, so I was pretty nervous once I neared the omnipresent warning signs that led up to it. Still, I expected that after the usual paperwork check, the soldiers would finally let me through, just as they had at the other two checkpoints on the way. Unfortunately, it didn't turn out to be that easy.

Approaching the checkpoint, I stopped the car at a concrete barrier designed to protect the soldiers manning the post from bullets, bombs, or any shady behavior from the natives.

"Your car…" said the soldier, pointing to the license plate at the front of my Polo, "It is an Israeli car. It can't go inside Nablus…*Momnooh, momnooh*," he laughed, using the one Arabic word that seemed to be a part of virtually every checkpoint soldier's linguistic repertoire: forbidden. This was as ridiculous as one could imagine. However, there were several places in the occupied territories that had this frustrating and incomprehensible rule. I just wished I'd thought to ask someone if Huwwara was one of them.

On one level, I could understand the supposed logic behind disallowing Palestinian cars inside Jerusalem and Israeli towns—it keeps out "the Arabs" (whether that meant it kept out the terrorists, the non-Jews, or the riffraff depended upon personal interpretation). But this odd reversal of the rule—supposedly to protect innocent Israeli citizens from driving into places like Nablus and getting into trouble (or much worse) was complete and clear bullshit. Jewish Israelis weren't exactly begging to drive their cars into downtown Nablus. Instead it was Israeli-Palestinians who were effectively barred from entering non-Israeli towns freely.

Shit, I thought. *I've come all this way for nothing.* There was no doubt about it. I would have to be brave, leave my car behind, and use my Arabic to its fullest capacity to brave Huwarra's public transportation. Yes, and I would do it, I vowed. But, as I was to find out, that was no small thing.

I parked my car in a small, fenced area that I hoped would be safe and I crossed through a walking security checkpoint. I passed through a long, chain-link chute and emerged into a huge, noisy melee of crowds, honking taxis, and men shouting destinations in the city that I had no chance of comprehending. Always finding it better to ask women for directions, I hurried over to a small group of college-aged girls and asked them the way to the city center taxis. There, I found one and settled into it with another woman, happily waiting for enough other passengers for us to depart.

Now, I normally have a better sense of social responsibility, such as waiting for my turn, etc. But there was something about this country on both sides of the Green Line that made embracing its residents' seemingly general disregard for lines and common courtesy uncommonly easy. So, when my co-passenger brought up the bright-idea to jump taxi and make for the next one with only two passengers till take-off, I happily made for the new car, full of passengers, idling, and ready to go. *Ah. That's better.* I smiled at my seatmate, and she winked at me in response.

Funny how it only takes a second for smugness to evaporate, though. As soon as the first, now jilted driver spotted us—his lost prey—he sprinted over to the taxi, ripped open the driver's door mid-acceleration, and hauled the man out like a light sack of potatoes. The car shuddered to a sudden stall.

Thankfully, and as usual in the West Bank, other men intervened before an all-out brawl could ensue, pulling the two drivers apart and forcing a quick reconciliation. With additional problems averted, the driver returned to the car, pulled out a cigarette, and screeched out of the lot, cursing the other driver loudly out the window.

Although my Arabic had been steadily improving, I still wasn't confident that I could navigate a new city with my linguistic handicap, no map, no car of my own, and—as I was just realizing in the car as we neared the city center—no cell phone. Uh oh. Even my phone's SIM card was "Israeli" and wouldn't function in Nablus. Still, there had to be a way to find Father Ibrahim, who, according to Omar, would be happy to point me the way to the church at Jacob's well and introduce me its resident priest.

After I got out in the city center, I calculated my next move. I didn't have a lot of time, and I certainly didn't want to go back through Huwwara at night, so I decided to find the fastest way to locate Father Ibrahim. Hunt down another Christian—and to do that, all I'd have to do was look for a sign...

People in the Holy Land love symbols of who they are. Golden Stars of David, Western and Eastern Crosses, and Quranic verses adorned the necks of the faithful (and the not-so-faithful) like nobody's business, to say nothing of the clothing styles that clearly identified the religion, and even politics, of the wearer.

Even the buildings often bore the mark of the owner or developer's religion or politics somewhere—from door plaques to traditional and funky mezuzahs and flags (Israeli towns make post 9/11 America look positively flagless in comparison). In Nablus, as well as in other Palestinian towns, this usually meant that finding a Christian Palestinian was about as easy as looking for the figure of St. George, the patron saint of Palestine, always on his steed, slaying a dragon in carved-stone relief upon the lintels of their homes and businesses.

Thankfully, I didn't have to walk far from where I'd gotten out of the taxi until I spotted George and his dragon adorning a small shop just off the main road, and I hurried over to what seemed to be a commercial tailor's shop. I walked in and approached a middle-aged woman sitting behind a large desk.

"*Marhaba*," I said, switching from my usual *Salaam* to the religiously neutral Arabic greeting. "I'm not from here…could you tell me where I could find the church of Father Ibrahim?"

I must have seemed more than odd. A foreign Muslim woman asking to see a priest in butchered Arabic? It's not like you encounter that every day in Nablus!

"*Ahlain*, Welcome," she answered, rising from behind the desk and walking around to get a better look at me.

She was middle-aged, short-haired and wearing slacks and a scoop-necked sweater, and she carried herself in the classy, confident, almost Sophia Loren-ish way I'd learned to associate with older Christian-Arab women. It was a blend of intelligence, pride, and attractive self-assurance (usually coupled with an excellent fashion sense), which came easier to these women. It distinguished them from their younger sisters, who seemed to prefer a more, shall we say, Fredericks of Hollywood style of dress.

"Where are you from?" she asked, introducing the usual litany of questions that my foreign demeanor always evoked—Why was I there? Where I did I live? Why did I want to see Father Ibrahim? (whom, thankfully, she knew.) Perhaps most important, was I married or not?

I did my best to answer her as quickly as I could, and though she still looked confused by me, and a little dubious about just what I was after, she carefully explained the directions to Father Ibrahim's church, which I wrote down quickly in transliterated Arabic, and headed out again on my way.

By the time I tracked down Father Ibrahim using the woman's directions, it was becoming late afternoon, and I was desperate to see the "miracle" body before I had to cut the day short and call the trip a bust. I still had three checkpoints to cross to get back home, and miles of windy, hilly roads through settler country.

Happily, Father Ibrahim understood my predicament, and after serving me the obligatory tea (and asking me the same questions as the dry cleaning lady), wasted no time in directing me to the site, which was in a much larger, and older walled church compound called Bir Yacoub, Arabic for Jacob's Well—thankfully, just down the road from where he lived.

Bir Yacoub is the site which Biblical Jacob purchased and camped on more than two thousand years ago. Today, a large, beautiful church is built over the deep well, which is situated in a cave-like crypt under the sanctuary floor. The well itself was definitely unusual, and when I peered down into its dark depths, I could clearly see the surface of the water, seemingly not more than twenty feet down. But when I threw in a coin, it took a full five seconds for it to hit the surface. It was then that the guard who took me down to the well told me "off the record" that the place is haunted. In fact, according to him, the water recently bubbled up to the rim clean and pure, at exactly the same moment the rest of the area's water supply became mysteriously tainted. Poisoned, he said…

Pretty cool story, I thought.

But, as I explained to him, I'd come to see the body.

A few steps up and out of the crypt and over to the right of the nave lay Archimandrite Philoumenos, the Greek Orthodox caretaker of the church, meters from where they found his body by the well, and only a week after a settler group had come to claim the site as a Jewish holy place. Although the killers were never convicted, the belief remained that it was a political/religious murder.

That was what got him there, encased in a glass box and on display for eternity. I did wonder if I was missing something, though, because the body was clearly decomposed—broken skull and all. Maybe I was lacking a certain faithfulness in my eyes, but all I saw was just another victim. It wasn't miraculous, or even inspiring. It was just a sad reminder of all those who have been murdered in what seemed to be an ageless—and hopeless—fight over holy land.

I hurried out, but not before getting a recommendation for the best *Kanafe* joint in town, where I bought ten kilos to go and headed back to Huwwara.

Thankfully, I make it back to the village without incident. I was exhausted, but proud of myself for going. Whether the well was miraculous or not, I didn't know (although I'd like to think so), and the dead priest on display was damn depressing. But one thing was for sure—something seemed to shift to the positive after the trip, as if I'd gained some sort of pilgramatic mojo.

Whatever the reason, my family crowded around in the living room when I got home—even my father-in-law! They were very curious about the details of my visit, listening intently to my story, and happily devouring the *Kanafe*. Clearly, they were adjusting to my trips out of Safa. In fact, the next time I returned to the village at night, following another evening visit to the Temple Mount with the kids, their only response was a demand from my sisters-in-law to take them along the next time.

To my surprise, no one resisted the idea, and I realized that the family's definition of what was acceptable for women might just be changing—a miracle to rival anything else I'd seen yet on my visits out and about in the Holy Land!

CHAPTER 21

This Land is Your Land...
This Land is My Land...

I like to see a man proud of the place in which he lives. I like to see a man live so that his place will be proud of him.

-ABRAHAM LINCOLN

When I'd left America, most people I told had been tactful enough to support my decision to take my kids to the region. It was only when I mentioned which side of the Green Line I was moving them to that some of them started to waffle. I was already feeling guilt, fear and insecurity about my choice and its impact on my mothering skills, so I didn't really welcome any negative input. So I quit calling it Palestine, or Israel, for that matter. I even quit mentioning Jerusalem. When new people found out about my plan, or I had to explain it for some reason, I found it much more comforting for all involved to call it something more, well, cozy: The Holy Land. It just sounded wholesome and wonderful, right? Who wouldn't want to take her children there?

The fact is, Palestine, Israel, the Holy Land, whatever you wanted or believed it should be called was more than a name. It had been the center of religious devotion since the beginning of recorded time. For me, my love of the Holy Land might have been a mental quirk akin to "Jerusalem Syndrome."

The kids were something different, though. They were half-Palestinian, and I felt they had a right to get to know the place as a literal home, a birthright, and I knew that waiting for a time when the conflict might someday end wasn't a reasonable option. In my heart of hearts I didn't really expect that day to ever come.

I came to this conclusion after spending time here. I knew that the reason why peace wouldn't likely arrive here was because of the continuing military occupation (now going on for more than forty-five years)—an occupation that made life so miserable for everyday Palestinians that they literally felt they had nothing to lose, including something so basic as hope. And it wasn't as simple as taking sides in the Israeli-Palestinian conflict, or even deciding if suicide bombings tipped the scales of suffering to the Israeli side. It was, as most Palestinians, and a growing number of Israelis were now saying—that the rusted, punitive military occupation made melding the two societies virtually impossible, for it was a machine that constantly turned out one constant and unwavering lesson to all it touched: the "other" was sub-human. This was the ugly, hate-filled reality that permeated the place: you can't make peace with animals.

I'd learned this fact so quickly because my pain threshold was pretty low compared to that of the Palestinians I lived among. Almost every Palestinian I knew in the village had seen a son beaten and dragged away by the military, had had their homes ransacked, been tear-gassed, and had been prevented from taking their children to the hospital when ill. They were even denied the right to travel (now, even to the Dead Sea)! But as awful as those things were, the real transformative power of the occupation was in the smaller, daily humiliations. Especially the checkpoints.

The main Jerusalem tunnel checkpoint is a perfect example—a large, modern, multi-lane structure that best resembled a wide toll crossing. It was all the more disarming for someone like me because of its modernity, as if it could have been transplanted on the New Jersey Turnpike. Although many Israelis would say that this checkpoint was necessary for "security," Palestinians call it a "machine of tyranny." The way it was set up was inconsistent; there didn't seem to be any rules. As a result, each individual soldier had the power to decide your fate that day based on his or her whim. If you needed to buy a dress for an upcoming wedding at a store on the other side of the checkpoint, say in East Jerusalem, it was essentially up to Zvi (who was probably pissed off at having to be in such a God-forsaken place to start with), whether you got that dress or not. So, too, if your child needed treatment at a clinic, or a group of school-children was headed out on a field trip, or you had an important meeting, it was up to the individual guard whether or not your plans would be approved.

I saw this as a set-up ripe for abuse, and the grossest examples came to light: A Palestinian man was forced to play his violin in front of the soldiers in exchange for passage, a child died of an asthma attack because his parents couldn't get him through the checkpoint in time, or a woman was forced to give birth at the side of the road (according to the United Nations, more than sixty Palestinian women have given birth at Israeli checkpoints since 2000, resulting in thirty-six deaths).

And that's not even considering the constant humiliation of having to plead your case. It was bad enough if you were alone—but believe me, there was little in this world that could create a searing hatred faster than having a teenager treat you like scum in front of your children. All of these things hurt both the Palestinians and the Israelis, for this phenomenon had begun the death knell of Israel's golden self-image. The much-heralded "Light Among Nations" was often found behaving like a common thug.

Still, some Israelis understood the tremendous damage that the checkpoints (and the occupation, itself) was doing to the long tradition of Jewish ethics, and to the eventual prospect of peace. Organizations like Peace Now, B'Tselem and Machsom Watch (made up almost entirely of older women) volunteered to stand and watch at the most infamous sites. As the organization's spokeswoman, Adi Dagan, explained their position in a 2004 *Mother Jones* article, "Grandmothers on Guard," "If they would just check people to make sure they're not carrying bombs, we wouldn't object...The problem is that the barriers serve as limitations on movement, and have a drastic effect on lives of Palestinians. Palestinians don't get to university, to work, to hospitals — the checkpoints totally disrupt civil life."

Take, for example, one of our earliest attempts to go to the Old City as a family. Whereas I could almost always pass the checkpoint, it was exponentially harder when the kids were along. It was not because they were security risks (at twelve, nine, and two), but because, as to the checkpoint soldier on guard often told me, "They are Arabs."

Still, it depended on the individual soldier, and I estimated that we could successfully pass the Tunnel Checkpoint about seventy percent of the time. In a few years, though, the percentage could dwindle to zero because according to the nebulous laws of the occupation, by the time my kids had reached high-school age and above, they would no longer be allowed to cross the major Israeli checkpoints. That meant no access to Jerusalem, or any place inside Israel, no small thing when you considered that Israel controlled all of the airports, borders, and even the Seas: Mediterranean, Red *and* Dead.

Sure, the Holy Land was still my oyster, and I could go where I pleased because I was classified as a tourist, just as any of the estimated 20,000 new Jewish immigrants from places as far-flung as Russia, France, and South Africa could go where they wished. This would not be so for my kids. If Amani, Ibrahim, and Karim, whose father's family traced its origins to the area back at least ten generations, were going to visit all of the Holy Land, time was definitely a'wastin'.

That's why when I visited the Temple Mount with the kids, I was determined to make as many good memories in the place as they could. The only catch was they were stuck with me, their linguistically challenged American mom, to show them the fairly complicated ropes. It wasn't the ideal situation, but it was the best I could offer, especially because nobody in my husband's family had the permit necessary to visit the city at all.

You couldn't just walk into the Temple Mount if you were a foreigner, and there was a large number of guards and police to keep errant tourists away from its hallowed grounds (after all, who knew what crazy antics we were capable of)? Even though I was a Muslim, and as such was officially allowed to visit freely, I had an unfortunate habit of losing my cool at the last moment. Somehow, I'd make sudden, shifty eye contact with whatever guard happened to be in my way.

It was always a ridiculous deer-in-the-headlights move—almost an involuntary tick; *Are you sure you wanna let me in?* My insecurity made me conspicuous, and I was always stopped and required to "prove" my religion by reciting verses of the Quran in Arabic to the Israeli policeman or woman (who were essentially the "outside" gatekeepers). Then, once I was inside the Mount, I'd have to repeat this with one of the Islamic guards on site.

Although it really wasn't a big deal; after all, I always managed to make it in—it was a process that always drew an audience, increasing my frustration—and my accent. And because I was always shy about my grasp of formal Arabic (the language of the Quran and somewhat akin to Shakespearean English), these quizzes were so embarrassing that I resolved to learn to fit in at the site enough to be ignored, a valuable skill I hoped to pass on to my kids.

It wasn't only the Arabic performances that made me want to blend in at the Mount, though. That award had to go to a little run-in I'd had with an angry mob over my use of Chapstick, about five years earlier when I went along on an outing with my mother and sister-in-laws to the old city for Friday prayers and a little shopping. It was also the day I had my first fight with Asya.

At the time, I thought that I was doing pretty well as I sat on the cool stones in the shade of the "Dome of the Chain," the mini open-air copy of the Dome of the Rock, where legend said King Solomon hung a chain that connected heaven and earth, and had the miraculous ability to "judge" between disagreeing parties. Although there is no evidence of the chain in modern times, I definitely could have used a little divine intervention that day.

It was the middle of Friday Prayers, the single most crowded, and possibly volatile, day of the week in the Old City—not the best time to call attention to yourself as an "American with attitude."

I wasn't praying that week (Muslim women are not expected to pray during that time of the month), so instead of going inside the hot, crowded Dome of the Rock, I decided to sit in the shade on the edge of the overflow crowd praying outside. My youngest sister-in-law, Sa'eda, had her three-month-old baby with her, and I volunteered to hold the baby while she prayed inside with the others.

Although I had found a spot in the shade, I realized I still had to hunch my back over the baby in order to shield him further from the intense midday sun. Unfortunately, in the act of doing so, the tip of my ponytail apparently peeked out from the back of my "hijab," because an older woman rushed over to tell me. Properly chastised, I quickly tucked in the offending strands.

It was hot, and as the prayer began I started to worry about the intensifying glare bouncing off the white paving stones that lined the surface of the Mount. Although I was mostly shaded, the sun was shifting and I needed to move. However, by then the crowd had grown large enough to make changing my location impossible, particularly because moving would have meant walking in front of the worshippers—an action that is absolutely forbidden. Thankfully, I could still shade the baby reasonably well with the edge of my scarf as I cradled him cross-legged on the ground. Unfortunately, I had another problem: the month before I'd begun treatment with the powerful (now, banned) drug, Accutane in order to get a stubborn case of acne under control.

As anyone who has tried it knows, Accutane is an amazingly effective but potentially deadly drug that, among other side effects, can make one extremely prone to sunburn and dry skin, to the tune of molting snake. As such, Accutane patients must wear protective clothing, sunscreen, and Chapstick anytime they are out in the sun or wind. I was wearing sunscreen, but as we had eaten lunch en route to the Mount, my lips were Chapstick free.

I had a trusty SPF 25 Chapstick in my purse—it's not as if I wasn't prepared for summer in the Middle East. The only problem was, in most Islamic societies it is considered extremely bad form to apply makeup of any kind in public. This is particularly true in conservative Palestine, and even more so during Friday prayers. Magnify that by sitting in the middle of the third holiest site in Islam, and you get the picture.

However, my horrific canker-sore episode was still fresh in my mind, my face was already peeling and I could literally feel the sun burning my lips. So I decided to take action, assuming that surely nobody would notice. Everyone was praying, for goodness sake! That meant they weren't looking at me, so I figured I'd stealthily pull out my Chapstick, hunch over, give my lips a quick swipe behind my hand, and nobody would be the wiser.

And that's where it all went wrong.

After a few minutes, the prayer ended and the crowd began to move off in several directions while I carried my nephew to one of the mosque entrances to await the others. As I walked toward the entrance of the building, an older woman touched my shoulder and quietly said, "Daughter, you know it is haraam (forbidden) to put on makeup."

Amazed that she had caught my stealthy lip-balming (wasn't she praying?), I smiled and nodded. I even thanked her. After all, I was still feeling pretty good about the day, and the woman was at that threshold age where she could pretty much tell me anything and I would treat her with respect. However, once I made it under the vaulted entrance to the Dome I joined a crowd of about fifty women sitting in the shade, obviously waiting to meet up with their groups, too. I stood there, shifting impatiently. The (breastfed) baby had started fussing, and the heat was getting to me. Where were my relatives?

As I stood there waiting, a woman in her early forties perched at the base of a stone pillar looked up at me and said, "I saw you putting on lipstick. You know, there are men that walk right though here, and it isn't good for you to do that."

Here we go, I thought wearily. Looking around, I noticed that most of the women milling around in the entrance had heard what she said and were looking right at me.

I smiled. After all, it was a silly misunderstanding, and responded, "Yes, I know...but it wasn't makeup...it's not lipstick...it's (Lord, how do you say "Chapstick" in Arabic?) medicine for lips. I even showed them the Chapstick (which was unfortunately the tinted kind). Yes, that's it, special medicine because..."

"No!" the first woman answered angrily (probably buoyed by my obvious foreignness once I opened my big, Arabic-challenged mouth). "I saw you! You put on lipstick right there in front of everyone!"

I sighed, my smile growing forced, and started to explain again. "No, I..."

"Yes, yes!" About five others also joined in, interrupting me and adding, "We saw you!"

Oh, my God! These crazy, sanctimonious, holier-than-thou...

It was then that Asya finally emerged from the mosque and into the excited crowd around me. As she made her way closer, I hurried to tell her what was going on. But the first woman, too impatient for me to finish my story, interrupted with her version of the scandal. When she finished, I repeated my story, stood back and relaxed, waiting for Asya to explain the situation to the women and get them off my back.

Instead, my loyal sister-in-law looked at them, smiled and announced, "But she is an American!"

Not good.

Open-mouthed, I turned to Asya, just in time to catch the hint of a smile on her treacherous face as the crowd erupted in exclamations of, "Tell her this isn't America!" and "You can't act like that here!"

Anger welled up in me, dissolving what logic and common sense I still possessed. There was something I sensed behind their words—a hate-tinged arrogance and willingness to attack me en masse, that ticked me off—that and the fact that there were plenty of other Arab women around us wearing heavy makeup, jeans, and other quasi-religious no-noes. Yet, they'd seized on me like a whore on the prowl in Vatican City.

But the final straw was when one young woman, twentyish and wearing the type of plain, chest-covering hijabs that identified her as an uber-religious local, joined the fray, piping up to add the final, shiny nugget, "We're just trying to teach her how to behave!"

As furious as I was with Asya for the way she let me twist in the wind, and devastated by what I felt was an attack on my "otherness," I shouted at them, "Why were you looking at me anyway, when you were supposed to be praying?"

Now I was drawing even more attention because of my accent. "It's because I'm an American, that's why—but you Arab women...all you do is yap yap yap..." I sniped, stabbing my hand out at them like a quacking duck for emphasis. "And you..." I continued, pointing at Miss Teach-Her-How-to-Behave, "You just shut your mouth and mind your own business!"

Suddenly, I realized that I could be teetering on the precipice of a serious beating—at the very least, with the "You Arab women" comment.

But it was just then, thankfully, that my mother-in-law emerged from the mosque and like a little, old, glorious deux ex machina, she took one look at the crowd, assessed the situation, and immediately went into righteous "Shame on you!" mode, chastising the crowd into silence and dragging me (by then wild-eyed and crying) and my sisters-in-law away, shouting behind her in awesome Arabic, "She's better than a hundred of you! May God curse your forefathers! Look at her, she wears the veil and she is Muslim, even though she is from America! Have you no shame?"

Yes! That's what I'm talkin' about!

Finally, we shuffled off toward one of the Mount's exits—me, a mess of blubbering, tear-wiping, self-pitying, Arab-hating "I wanna go home" thoughts, and my mother-in-law and two sisters-in-law in wide-eyed shock. Asya, too, was blubbering after I tongue-lashed her for her "She's an American!" comment and her snide smile.

If my "Mount Chapstick" experience taught me the importance of blending in, I also learned that there was a whole other set of criteria that applied to me because I was an outsider. (And yes, I also realized it is better to control one's temper when surrounded by a crowd). It was important to fit in if only to avoid problems and misunderstandings—plus, it just plain hurt to be singled out. I swore that next time, I'd blend.

I consciously changed my personal style in the years following the incident, slowly morphing from typical American-Muslim look (long skirts, long sleeve shirts, and a long, oblong wrapped scarf), to West Bank style, mimicking the Islamic clothing trends that came hot off the Muslim catwalks (yes, they existed) and though I certainly knew that clothing alone didn't "make the woman," I wasn't above using it as a cloak of armor.

My new *modus operandi* was to dress the part. Now, I wore traditional or contemporary Arabic styles of Islamic dress, specifically, the long trench-coat like garments known as *jilbabs*, or the much more comfy black, voluminous *abaya*—all the rage that season in shiny satin, with oversized Moroccan hoods, trimmed with tassels. I even used them as a kind of camouflage that I wore into the mosques back in America, once I realized it could shield me from the "let's humiliate the convert" game—a popular sport at the Northwest mosques I attended.

Indeed, it seemed that many of the expatriate Muslims in our area had skills of Olympic quality, for they could make the occasional new, hopeful interloper run from the congregation faster than a hare from a pack of hyenas. After all, how would you feel if someone went out of her way to point out that your prayers wouldn't be accepted by the Almighty because you had fingernail polish on, or watched you while you prayed just in case you needed some direction on the proper way to do it. Apparently, converts like me could only be counted on to find the faith, stand up to their non-Muslim families (who are usually unhappy with the transformation, sincere or no), and learn a totally new way of worship.

But getting respect was a whole other matter, and it was even harder in Palestine. Palestinian society was still relatively homogenous, especially in the smaller West Bank villages. People like me, Muslim or no, were still *ajaneb* (foreigners) perched on a branch of the family tree so weak it threatened to snap with the slightest move. If I always felt my position in the community and the family was precarious, that was one thing. I chose this life. But I desperately wanted to save Ibrahim, Amani, and Karim from a similar fate. I wanted my kids to belong to their community, and their family.

One of the first things that surprises visitors to the Temple Mount is the way it opens from the narrow, crowded, and dark alleyways and passages crisscrossing the Old City into a bright, wide vista of green pine, cedar, olive trees and flowering rhododendron, crowned at its center by the bright gold Dome of the Rock.

It's a sight meant to impress, and one so beautiful it rivals the Western Wall as the image most associated with the Jewish state. It is either protected until Judgment Day (as many Muslims believed) or will someday be destroyed, to be replaced by a new temple (as some Christians and most religious Jews hoped), but for now locals and tourists admire the view, history, and sanctity of the place, regardless of religious affiliation. After all, according to Jewish tradition, it was here that the divine presence of God rested, an idea that the beauty of the place made it all the easier to believe.

If dressing the part was vital to being able to experience the Temple Mount as I wanted, acting the part had its place as well (and you sure as hell wouldn't catch me whipping out anything resembling makeup there again). Now, on this visit to the Holy Land, I finally felt I was catching on enough to be as invisible as the locals. This was no small accomplishment for an Oregon mom with three high-spirited kids in tow.

Ninety percent of the difficulty of getting into the Mount with the kids hinged on avoiding the Israeli police outside the gates, the odds of which improved significantly once I lectured the kids against speaking at all within earshot of the officers. If we could avoid that hurdle, I found we were usually able to circumvent the interrogation reserved for foreigners completely, leaving us free to roam the site uninterrupted.

It might have seemed strange that the kids would have loved the Mount. After all, the place is so touchy that the only behavior I'd seen from the non-Muslim visitors from the four corners of the world was hushed, fearful reserve. It was the nature of the place because of the so-called "status quo" agreement made after the Israeli conquest of the city in 1967. Afterwards, then Prime Minister Levi Eshkol vowed that "no harm whatsoever shall come to the places sacred to all religions."

Therefore, the inside of the Mount generally remained under the control of the Islamic authorities, while access to the Mount itself was up to the Israeli police outside. And that meant no young Palestinian men were allowed (unless they were locals with Jerusalem IDs), foreigners were restricted to one designated entrance and subject to limited visiting hours, and religious Jews or Christians were prohibited from praying, bringing in religious texts (including Bibles), or even singing. All of the complexity and gravity of the place meant that most visitors walked in somber, tight little groups, speaking in hushed tones to avoid any rebuke. The one exception to this general rule of decorum, however, was generally granted to children—and for my kids, that was a powerful draw.

Although I had a limited church background growing up, I didn't recall being allowed to make a ruckus. Yet the Temple Mount—the most jealously guarded religious site in the world—was one place where at least the kids could cut loose. They were allowed the run of the entire compound, from the site of Fort Antonia on the northern end, to the far walls abutting the black-domed Al Aqsa mosque. In particular, they loved the "cool places," their favorite spots that they demanded we visit every time. This began in the cave under the Dome of the Rock, where they pressed their ears to the floor above the "Well of Souls" and tried to hear the spooky whispers rumored to waft up from the covered opening. It is a place Mark Twain (in his day, lucky enough to get in) described in his work, *Innocents Abroad*, a characteristically humorous account of his 1867 pilgrimage to the Holy Land:

> The great feature of the Mosque of Omar is the prodigious rock in the center of its rotunda. It was upon this rock that Abraham came so near offering up his son Isaac—this, at least, is authentic—it is very much more to be relied on than most of the traditions, at any rate. On this rock, also, the angel stood and threatened Jerusalem, and David persuaded him to spare the city. Mahomet was well acquainted with this stone. From it he ascended to heaven. The stone tried to follow him, and if the angel Gabriel had not happened by the merest good

luck to be there to seize it, it would have done it. Very few people have a grip like Gabriel—the prints of his monstrous fingers, two inches deep, are to be seen in that rock to-day.

This rock, large as it is, is suspended in the air. It does not touch anything at all. The guide said so. This is very wonderful. In the place on it where Mahomet stood, he left his foot-prints in the solid stone. I should judge that he wore about eighteens. But what I was going to say, when I spoke of the rock being suspended, was, that in the floor of the cavern under it they showed us a slab which they said covered a hole which was a thing of extraordinary interest to all Mohammedans, because that hole leads down to perdition, and every soul that is transferred from thence to Heaven must pass up through this orifice...

Next, the kids and I would almost always walk down the wide stairs from the upper platform down to the black-domed Al Aqsa building, open, bright, and somehow friendlier than the gloomy Dome of the Rock, where Karim loved to chase the fat doves waddling along the carpets up to the rafters. Amani and Ibrahim, too, particularly loved this place because of its perfectly kid-sized cubbyhole windows, where they would cozy up to watch groups of Christian and Jewish faithful singing far below the ancient grilles.

But hands down, the kids loved their usual last stop best - a cavernous, second century Roman water reservoir-turned-mosque then Crusader stable, and then mosque again - mostly because there they could join the local, Old City kids in what seemed to be a perpetual game of tag. It was called Solomon's Stables, or the Marwani Mosque.

The kids loved the place for all the light-hearted fun they had there, but the fact still remained that it was one of the most jealously contested places in the world. The center of Jewish faith and history, the third holiest site in Islam, and perhaps most important, the site where Jews,

Christians and Muslims believe the Messiah will one day appear, it was thirty-five acres of "it's mine," from before Roman times. And although it was beautiful, peaceful, and welcoming, you were always aware of the gravity of the place. The Mount demanded respect.

CHAPTER 22

Where Angels are Forbidden to Tread

…Thus violent deeds live after men upon the earth, and traces of war and bloodshed will survive in mournful shapes long after those who worked the desolation are but atoms of earth themselves.

— CHARLES DICKENS

Blame it on one too many Indiana Jones movies, but of the things I really loved about Jerusalem, indeed the whole country, was the fact that it was often just plain creepy. There were stories of the Crusader massacres in Jerusalem, when witnesses reported that the heart of the Old City was awash in Jewish, Muslim, and even Eastern Christian blood up to the knees of the victor's war horses, and the story of Mamilla Pool, a huge stone reservoir constructed by Herod the Great during the first century BCE in the heart of a Muslim cemetery. Today, it's virtually hidden in plain sight, directly across from the US consulate! Even more bizarre, it's surrounded by broken chain-link fencing, scattered garbage, and used syringes from the drug addicts who've found it a convenient spot to shoot up.

I visited the place a few times, and it was always completely deserted, a clearing in the heart of what was becoming the trendy part of town, complete with a new pedestrian mall sporting Rolex, Crocs, and Gap stores, the newest additions to the ancient landscape. It was a weird place, though, and was recently the site of a supremely ironic and controversial new museum, the Simon Wiesenthal Center's Museum of Tolerance, constructed atop the Muslim cemetery (bodies dug up and all). It was also home to one of the largest, yet least known, massacres in the city's history.

It was hard not to get caught up in the site's grisly story, which I first read about in a 2006 *Jerusalem Post* article by Israeli columnist, Gil Zohar. I learned that there, in the spot where I was standing, an estimated 60,000 people had been slaughtered in "the killing field of 614."

In a classic Jerusalem outcome, three hundred years of Byzantine Christian rule ended when the Persians invaded Palestine and took Jerusalem after a twenty-day siege. According to Zohar:

> ...Once Jerusalem was in Persian hands a terrible massacre of Christians took place, and the Jews are accused of having taken the lead in this massacre...How many Christian prisoners of war were murdered by the Mamilla Pool? A precise number is of course now impossible to verify, but Israeli archaeologist Ronny Reich puts the tally at 60,000 before the Persian military stopped the carnage. One eyewitness, Strategius of St. Sabas, wrote: "Jews ransomed the Christians from the hands of the Persian soldiers for good money, and slaughtered them with great joy at Mamilla Pool, and it ran with blood."

Today, the only evidence of the massacre is a burial cave discovered in 1992 by a construction crew working on a parking lot. On the entrance, they found a Greek inscription reading, "Only God Knows Their Names." Inside, they found it filled with thousands of bones (mostly women and children, because many of the men were away fighting the Persians elsewhere in the country).

And although many Israelis and diaspora Jews seemed to be uncomfortable with the story, perhaps feeling that it was damaging PR even after 1,400 years, others like Judith Mendelsohn Rood, Professor of History and Middle Eastern Studies at Biola University, suggested that "… believers in the God of Abraham, Jews, Muslims and Christians together should hallow the blood-soaked ground of Mamilla."

After all, as Professor Rood pointed out, "The importance of the archaeological research isn't only to understand the history of the land and to verify the truth of the facts we know from our sources, but…sheds light on the development of human culture. Therefore, its importance overrides nations and borders."

I thought it sounded like a great plan. It was certainly more appropriate than building a Museum of Tolerance dedicated solely to the plight of the Jewish people, yet built upon the destroyed remains of their Muslim neighbors. But then again, that was Jerusalem.

The day I visited the pool, alone, and with pepper spray firmly in hand, I made my way through the cemetery, carefully walking over a carpet of old pine needles and dust as I kept a sharp eye out for the discarded syringes littering the sinking graves and crumbling mausoleum. Finally, I came upon a broken fence surrounding the old pool, and looked down into the stone expanse, now dry and overgrown in the reddish light.

I soon found a large enough hole to squeeze through and descended into the pool, wandering across its floor, imagining how it must have looked on the day when so many people were slaughtered here, looking up helplessly at the Jerusalem sky.

I think one way to regard religion is as one big Ghost Hunter's episode, where we have an intense desire to know that there's more to this world than meets the eye, and that maybe all of the pain we have to experience in life actually means something. Still, in the Holy Land, this quest for meaning has too often led to atrocities, racism, and cruelty. What many outsiders don't understand is that the history of the place has produced a legacy that endures today, regardless of the strife that accompanied it.

The place was called Topheth, Gehenem, or just plain Hell. Located in the valley of Hinnom, just southwest of the Old City, it is believed to be the location where the Canaanites sacrificed their children to a god named Moloch, symbolized by a large metal statue/god fashioned in the shape of an immense bull. According to Rashi, a twelfth century French rabbi:

> Tophet is Moloch, which was made of brass; and they heated him from his lower parts; and his hands being stretched out, and made hot, they put the child between his hands, and it was burnt; when it vehemently cried out; but the priests beat a drum, that the father might not hear the voice of his son, and his heart might not be moved.

Eventually the practice of child sacrifice fell out of favor as the older, pagan religions were replaced by Judaism. But even then the valley was cursed to remain a place of darkness and filth; it was a large, constantly burning cesspool of dead bodies, animal carcasses, offal, and refuse from the city. According to the Hebrew Bible, or the Tanakh, "They have built the high places of Topheth...to burn their sons and their daughters in the fire. On account of this abomination Topheth and the Valley of Hinnom should be called "The Valley of Slaughter", for they shall bury in Topheth, till there be no place to bury." (Jeremiah 7:31-32).

The day I took the kids and Manar to see it, though, we were surprised to find only a beautiful, grassy meadow punctuated by ancient olive trees sending their roots deep into the soot and bloodstained soil below. It actually turned out to be an awesome place for a picnic...and as we sat on the grassy ground over what was the most despised locations on earth, I said a prayer for the souls of the victims, and hugged Karim tight—listening to the wind rustle through the trees as if to sigh for the pain this site had once absorbed.

There seemed to be an inexhaustible supply of sites like Topheth; these were places that sparked the imagination and forced people to confront the history behind many of their long-held beliefs. It was the same urge, I'd wager, that prompted many pilgrims, the faithful and the curious to flock to the Holy Land over the millennia, trying to extract Jerusalem's deepest secrets, oftentimes with the goal of somehow "proving" that their religious outlook was the "right" one.

It was with this kind of determination that one of the greatest Holy Land explorers to come out of the West was born. He was a *real* Indiana Jones, by the name of Sir Charles Warren.

Warren was an officer and archaeologist in The British Royal Engineers in the late nineteenth century and was fascinated by the underground structures—the basement level, if you will— of the Temple Mount. Famous in his day for his work as the former head of the London Police and especially for working the Jack the Ripper case, Warren and his partner, Charles Wilson, were recruited by the Palestine Exploration Fund (PEF), an organization founded under the auspices of Queen Victoria in 1865. Its purpose was to promote research into "the archaeology, history, manners, customs and culture, topography, geology, and natural sciences of Biblical Palestine and the Levant." This was actually a convoluted way of saying what they were really doing—using their Bibles, measuring tape, and survey equipment in a quest for definite proof of the Christian faith, an activity Warren dubbed "biblical archaeology reconnaissance." Of course, maybe finding a treasure or two wouldn't hurt, either.

Although Warren managed several dangerous and often stealthy major excavations close to the south-eastern walls of the Old City, his most significant "discoveries" were the underground tunnels and structures beneath the Temple Mount, about which he penned several letters that would later become a journal of his adventures. It was in these letters that Wilson described what it was like to undertake "sneaky archaeology"—explorations of forbidden sites that were scientific, but also had elements of a spy mission/religious quest. Whatever Wilson's true motivations, the work was daring and incredibly difficult, often conducted in semi-secret, without flashlights, safety harnesses, or climbing equipment. Worse, much of the expedition was conducted in winter, making the work in the wet, cold underground even more challenging. As Wilson wrote about his descent into one of the chambers:

> On lighting up the magnesium ire and looking about me, I was astonished, my first impression being that I had got into a church similar to that of the cathedral (formerly a mosque) at Cordova. I could see arch upon arch to north and east, apparently rows of them....On the cement a number of white hands were painted, probably as a charm against evil spirits...After floundering about some little distance, however, I could see that there was a limit to these substructures at no great distance to north and east. In the meantime Sergeant Birtles was making great efforts above with very little result; do what he would he could not get past the narrow opening to the cistern, and at last had to give up the trial and go and get leave from the owner to pull down the upper mouth of the shaft, and then he very soon appeared at the bottom, his shoulders considerably injured in his exertions. In the meantime the excitement of our "find" had begun to wear off, and the water felt cold. I was just giving the sergeant some sage advice as to how he could direct his steps to the best advantage, when I stumbled over a large stone and fell into the water flat on my face. As just as present the weather is frosty, and the rain is

generally accompanied by sleet or hail, a bath in one's clothes is anything but pleasant...

I was surprised when I first read Wilson's work. After all, I'd been to the Temple Mount several times and I'd never heard mention about these places—it seemed to me impossible that anything of real size could be found beneath the platform. But that's when I came across an old oil painting of the largest of these "secret chambers," (although, back then, well-known to locals) known simply as the Great Sea, painted by the water colorist, William Simpson, who worked with the Fund during the same time as Wilson.

There was just something about that painting that captured my imagination, along with the fact that despite numerous searches, I hadn't been able to come up with a single photograph of the place. In fact, it seemed that Wilson and his surveyors were the last Westerners to see the underground structures; after them, there was no further mention of them, as if they didn't exist at all. It didn't take much research for me to discover the reason behind this dearth of new information, descriptions, or photographs of the sites Wilson described.

Everything on the Mount—its features, history, measurements, access to archaeological exploration, whatever—was a forbidden subject. That was because both the Israelis and the Palestinians were terrified that the other might find some remains or archeological evidence supporting their particular religious belief. Perhaps the Temple was located in such or such a place, and therefore the Dome of the Rock must be destroyed to make way for it. Or perhaps the Islamic authorities on the sight might discover some fabulous artifact, such as the Ark of the Covenant. Just the same, many believed that poking around under stuff just wasn't a good idea in general (especially in the Holy Land, where there are scorpions under those rocks). They were concerned that it could change the future of who ultimately "got to keep" Jerusalem in the long run.

For centuries across the Western World, the Temple Mount was considered to be the literal center of the universe, and was used for religious purposes by the Jews, Romans, Muslims, and Christians for thousands of years. It was the site where Abraham was said to have prepared to sacrifice his son, Isaac, and where the First Temple was destroyed by the Babylonians in 586 BCE, as well as the Second Temple destroyed by the Romans in 70 CE. It is also where, according to Biblical tradition, the third and final Temple will be built one day.

The Mount is the point toward which religious Jews turn during prayer, but is considered so holy that many of them will not walk on its surface at all, lest they inadvertently enter the area still imbued with the Divine Presence of God.

Today, Muslims also consider the site to be holy—third only after Mecca and Medina in Saudi Arabia. Islamic, Jewish and Christian faithful share many of the same prophets and prophetic stories with which the sites are associated (with small differences of detail—Abraham prepared to sacrifice Ishmael, not Isaac, as in the Biblical story, for example). It is also mentioned in the Koran as the "Farthest Mosque" from which Muhammad ascended to heaven on his "Night Journey" to lead the other prophets who came before him (including Adam, Moses, and Jesus).

In fact, all of the structures and the land within the Mount are considered to be "the mosque" referred to in the Quran. And the black-domed Aqsa building on the southern side of the Mount is distinguished as one of the oldest Islamic buildings in the world.

The more I thought about Simpson's painting and read Wilson's journals, the more obsessed I became with a need to see them. The problem was, I knew there was no way a foreign female American with pitiful Arabic skills and a huge chip on her shoulder could possibly gain access. Still, I pored over Wilson's maps and drawings, reading all of his descriptions of the tanks, cisterns, and chambers. It was then that I came across an old engraving of the inside of the Golden Gate (Mercy Gate in Arabic). This was the immense, walled-up double arched passageway leading from the Mount of Olives to the to the Temple Mount through which people (and, according to Jewish tradition, the Divine Presence of God) passed.

The next time I was on the Mount, I made a point of ending my usual walk around the quiet, wooded area beneath the platform so I could look at the Golden Gate. There, I saw a long flight of stairs descending onto a wide, arched courtyard where the gate stood, built into the wall like an immense closed portico. As always, the area was deserted. I stayed there for a few minutes, caressed by a gentle breeze that rustled through the olive trees—and felt something that reminded me of peace.

There was only one problem—the Golden Gate and the underground chambers weren't open to the public. In fact, the large gated building was locked and "sealed," strictly off-limits to all but a select few of the Islamic authority in charge of the site. Still, the more I thought about it, the more I felt I needed to get inside—partly to see if I could. The Mercy Gate was literally a place where almost nobody had the right to be.

It suddenly occurred to me that the combination of my chosen faith and the indelible otherness that I'd fought so hard to erase over the years, might actually be a strength for once in my life. Maybe my outsider status would actually work in my favor.

I just hadn't quite figured out how.

Left: Amani (in a "tagim salah" or prayer outfit required on the mount), Karim and Ibrahim exploring the Eastern Wall and ramparts from the Temple Mount. Above: The immediate family, Safa, 2014.

Above: Exterior view of the Dome of the Rock. Right: Karim, Amani and Ibrahim exploring the Dome of the Chain the "mini" Dome of the Rock (now closed for renovations).

Manar, sidekick extraordinaire, at the Dome of the Rock during the evening prayer. Now, as an older teenager, she is forbidden from entering Jerusalem.

Above: View from the roof of "the castle," our home. Below: The view from our neighborhood in Safa toward the Mediterranean Sea.

Above: View from the top of the Eastern Wall toward the Mount of Olives where Jesus is expected to return. View to the Church of All Nations. Right: Army tower and gate used to close the village.

Part
Four

All Roads to War

CHAPTER 23

Beautiful Day for a War

Lights of ships moved in the fairway—a great stir of lights going up and going down. And farther west on the upper reaches the place of the monstrous town was still marked ominously on the sky, a brooding gloom in sunshine, a lurid glare under the stars.

-JOSEPH CONRAD

It was on a sunny, unseasonably warm day in the end of December, and the kids were playing outside with their cousins. I could hear them joining into the Arabic conversation with the blustery vocabulary of the very young. To my relief, they were truly bonding with their cousins—Ibrahim joining in with the boys playing Jaish and Shebab, the local version of cowboys and Indians, Amani playing "school" with the girls, and Karim, always joined by his two cousins, Ahmad and Muhammad. The little boys, aged four and five, had big, dark brown cartoon-cute eyes and could empty my cookie jar faster than a thirsty horse can drain a bucket. Together, the three of them were an awesome force. Now, looking back on that day, I'm convinced it was its peaceful comfort that made what was to happen seem even more horrific.

I was standing next to the open windows in my kitchen, enjoying the breeze and sunshine after days of frigid cold. Manar was visiting, looking up something on my computer, and I was washing dishes and lamenting the loss of my beloved coffee press after dropping it on the tile floor. That's when we heard it—the sound of fighter jets streaking across the sky. Although it was normal to have a constant hum of military aircraft above the West Bank, the sudden volume told us that something had to be very wrong. It only took one look between us for us to both to sprint for the stairs to an upper balcony, where we could better see what was going on.

We stood, silent and unbelieving, and watched the planes streak by, leaving vapor trails like nasty snags in the satin-blue sky—and as they left our line of sight, they were replaced by a sound I'd never heard before: the deep, horrifying percussion of a bombardment more than thirty-five miles away.

It was December 27, 2008, and The Gaza War had begun.

CHAPTER 24

The Sky is Falling

Teacher bought a big top for me
Solid (cast) lead, the finest known.
In whose honor, for whose glory?
For Hanukkah alone.

-HN Bailik

I t was as if life simply stopped for everyone during those first few hours of the war, which we were then learning already had a name: Operation Cast Lead, so named by the Israeli government in honor of the seventh day of Hanukkah, the day the war began, and taken from a poem by H.N. Bailik that refers to a cast lead dreidel, the spinning top traditionally played with during the holiday.

Fearing that the war would also extend to the West Bank, I hurried to the store to stock up on essential supplies before they could run out; propane, water, oil, flour, boxed milk and cans of tuna; you could live on these for a long time if you had to…but when I got to the grocery store, there wasn't a run on anything. Instead, everyone was frozen, looking grimly up at the store's ceiling-mounted television, which was streaming in images from Gaza so grisly I had to turn away. Still, as I loaded up my basket, I could hear them talking about the "new bombs" that I saw flashing across the screen, bombs that burst out like white fireworks raining down tiny smoke particles onto people running in the street. They even used the English words, as if the name were too new to be in Arabic: White Phosphorous.

It seemed too horrible to be true, especially for a weapon that was actually pretty. Designed to be used as a smoke shield, or in limited field applications, it wasn't supposed to be used on populated civilian areas. But there it was, on constant replay on Al-Jazeera, CNN, and even Fox News. Conventional bombs and bullets were responsible for far more deaths than during those first few days than from injuries sustained by White Phosphorous. However, it was the nature of the weapon—its ability to stick to the skin and burn flesh until it was deprived of oxygen or dug out of the wound, that seemed to add a psychological effect that was impossible to deny.

By evening, normal life had virtually stopped across the West Bank, and everyone stayed huddled around their televisions. Gaza remained under direct bombardment, followed by riots across the West Bank protesting the disproportionate amount of civilian deaths and the inhumane nature of some of the weapons being used. If we thought the White Phosphorus was freaky, rumors abounded of another, even more obscure "phantom weapon," one so new that few people in the world knew it existed, let alone what it was made of, or what it could do. All that we knew for sure was that if the latest reports from hospitals in Gaza were true, something had been let loose on Gaza that might be straight out of a science fiction movie.

If the hospitals and health care were considered abominable in the West Bank, all reports said that they were much worse in Gaza. Months of sanctions against the Hamas-led government had made essential supplies and medicines hard to come by before the war, but once the bombardment started what few resources they had become woefully inadequate. Still, there was a handful of primarily Norwegian doctors in Gaza at the time of the conflict, but they were as stymied by the lack of supplies, power interruptions and all of the other complications inherent in war. What they could do, however, was report on a new type of injury that they were seeing among the casualties, something experts on CNN and other news networks were just starting to associate with a weapon called DIME.

This was a new kind of device developed in the United States that was (according to its developers), "designed to minimize collateral damage." This might have been true back in the laboratory, but its damage to the psyche couldn't be overestimated. The international medical community was reporting that victims were arriving at the hospital with horrific cauterized amputations. According to the famous *Goldstone Report* on the war:

> The amputations mostly occurred at waist height in children, generally lower in adults, and were combined with skin-deep, third-degree burns, four to six fingers upward from the amputation. Where the amputation took place, the flesh was cauterized as a result of the heat. The patients with these amputations had no shrapnel wounds, but red flashes on the abdomen and chest. The excision of large pieces of flesh was not infrequent in these patients.

Reports like this started flowing out of Gaza with sickening frequency, and Mads Gilbert, one of the Norwegian doctors who first blew the whistle about them, told reporters that he had a "very strong suspicion" that Gaza was being used as a test laboratory for new weapons, and that he'd seen similar injuries during his work at Gaza's Shifa hospital. He reported seeing "a number of very brutal amputations...without shrapnel injuries which we strongly suspect must have been caused by the DIME weapons."

In just the span of a single day, it seemed as if the world—and her principles—had suddenly changed, and the Holy Land was now a frightening place for very different reasons than before.

As the days passed, Israeli forces swarmed the West Bank's cities, roads and villages in unusually high numbers as a show of force. This was to deter the rest of Palestine from joining in the fight. Still, large riots popped up in virtually every Arab city and town, from the North of Israel to the southernmost edge of the West Bank, especially in Hebron.

Hebron was always a volatile town, both because of its infamous settlement problem populated with five hundred of "the most hardened, racist, assholes you'd ever be so lucky to meet" (and that was according to other Israelis) and because of the Palestinian locals' infamous "Hebronian hard-headedness." After the war started, it only got worse. Still, I continued to teach my English classes in the newer part of town, where it was almost completely removed from the continuous demonstrations since the first day of the war.

 But the truth was, I'd always wanted to go to a real demonstration; the kind you see on CNN—burning tires, bullets, tear gas, rock throwing, banners—the works. After all, it seemed so worldly! So, one day before class, I made up my mind to check out the demonstration going on downtown.

Now, here I was on the edge of Old Hebron a couple of hours before class, speed-walking in my sober-looking work *jilbab* and Sketchers (just in case I had to run), headed toward the alleys that made up the marketplace next to the city's outdoor market. I'd parked my car as soon as I'd reached the city center, its shops and storefronts shuttered and locked, the garbage-strewn streets all the more depressing for their lack of usual crowds, shunning the prospect of an accidental stoning.

Still, I was there. I'd come to see, and I was going to see it all, damn it. However, my enthusiasm started to flag as soon as I hit the first wave of tear gas on the edge of the crowd (which I only then noticed was exclusively male). I wasn't accustomed to the sensation, which can sneak up on you well before you see the tell-tale cloud. Still, I wanted to get as close to the front line as I could, so I imitated the males ahead of me, hugging the edge of the closed storefronts to avoid getting hit by the rifle-fired gas grenades.

There was no question about it. The tear gas hurt— just like it was supposed to. But I realized that if I stayed out of the clouds of concentrated smoke as much as possible, I could still tolerate it—just barely. What I didn't appropriately estimate, though, was the sheer noise of the crowd, the terrifying, bone-jarring volume of the stun grenades, and the Crack! Ping! of the bullets. Worse, when I did make it to the front of the crowd, I couldn't really see the soldiers at all because they were crouched far beyond a concrete barrier, which made it hard to gage the direction of the greatest danger. Since I couldn't tell the exact angles from where the shots and gas rockets were coming from, I decided to muster up some belated common sense and crouch snugly in a side alley. From here, I could watch the mayhem unfold, until a roving group of Palestinian teenagers and boys discovered me. They assumed I was lost and offered to lead me out of the area.

I'd hoped to stay inconspicuous and especially didn't want to advertise my American roots, as I'd just seen two foreign journalists chased out of the area for taking pictures of the demonstrators, but thankfully, it was one of the days that my nationality didn't matter, and the kids welcomed me enthusiastically after I told them that I was an American Muslim. Still, it wasn't long before I realized that my presence seemed to encourage the boys to show off with increasingly risky antics: running into the line of fire to hurl stones, flip the bird (inverted, Arabic-style), or shaking their asses in the direction of the assembled troops, typical behavior, except that some of the boys were so young they exposed their superhero underpants when they crouched down to break cinderblocks into "ammunition." A vision of one of them getting their heads blown open trying to impress me flashed through my mind, and I knew it was time to get out of there.

I turned and tried to head back the way I came, still staying as close to the buildings as I could, but by then the tear gas was as thick and low in the street as a lingering river fog, and there was just no getting through it. Desperate, I tried using one of the raw onions the boys around me were holding up to their noses in a futile effort to counteract the gas. However, the moisture from my tears, even the sweat on my forehead, seemed to concentrate the agent on my skin as if I'd rubbed a jalapeño all over my eye-sockets, cheekbones, and lips. It was only when a gas rocket streaked past my foot, missing me by fewer than five inches, that I decided it was time to beat it back to work, even if I had to crawl blindly back to my car. I'd had enough excitement for the day.

Later, after getting home, I went straight to the shower to wash off any remaining gas residue and hurried to prepare the Kosher hot dogs I always kept in the freezer for unexpectedly long days. As I watched the children huddled around the *Soba* with their nutritious hot dogs and cups of soda, I started to feel guilty for putting myself at unnecessary risk. The thought had the very unpleasant effect of making me doubt the whole enterprise of being here, as if I somehow lacked the good judgment to stay. After all, the truth of the situation was that I'd found the demonstration scary, but also, strangely fun.

That night, as if in divine retribution for my folly, my hands started to hurt in a way I could only describe as the kind of nerve pain you get when you hit your funny bone. I only felt it in both of my wrists, hands and fingers, and it seemed to occur when I lay down or let my hands hang at my sides (in other words, all the time). In fact, the only relief I could get was when I slept, or if I sat up with my hands on top of my head. It was horrible. In fact, I had to take prescription pain killers just to get to sleep, and it felt (as best as I could describe it to the doctor), was as if the bones in my hands were melting.

Worse than the pain, though, was the thought that it started the night of the demonstration, where I'd allowed myself to remain in the teargas for at least an hour. I hadn't been injured, shot, or hit with any-thing, and that fact only increased my fear. *What on earth was in that gas?* After all, if they were using new, freaky weapons over the hills in Gaza, wouldn't they spike the gas with something? I didn't know if I was being paranoid or realistic. Maybe it was just an allergic reaction.

Thankfully, after a few days the pain finally stopped as suddenly as it started, leaving no trace behind…aside from a permanently numb finger and the important lesson that its best to *try* and stay out of trouble!

CHAPTER 25

Tamar

Illusions commend themselves to us because they save us pain and allow us to enjoy pleasure instead. We must therefore accept it without complaint when they sometimes collide with a bit of reality against which they are dashed to pieces.

-SIGMUND FREUD

Tamar was my Israeli neighbor back in Seattle, and though it confused our respective spouses, we'd become fast friends after she invited me to her home one day for tea. While it's true we disagreed on the Israeli/Palestinian conflict—and who was at fault—or at least who should back off *now*—we still managed to bond over our shared outsider statuses; she, the stereotypical blunt Israeli, and me, the scary Muslim. It was actually a nice relationship; she taught me to make proper schnitzel in her bright kitchen, and I gave her spices and taught her how to make Palestinian sage-infused tea. My kids swam with hers in her pool—and we even babysat for each other.

By the time I was back in Palestine, Tamar had returned to her home in northern Israel and I decided that since we were in the same country again, we could arrange to meet in Jerusalem. So I sent her an email and we arranged to meet a week later.

Like many secular Israelis, Tamar was a bit spooked by Jerusalem and its network of confusing neighborhoods, so we arranged to meet at the Jerusalem Promenade, a large pedestrian park overlooking a beautiful vista of the Old City. We thought maybe we'd head over to the mall in West Jerusalem, where we could have coffee and catch up on all that we'd missed in each other's lives during the months we'd spent apart.

As usual, going to Jerusalem meant passing through the Tunnels checkpoint south of the city, but because I didn't have the kids with me, I expected to pass through relatively quickly after the usual paperwork and trunk checks.

Unfortunately, that day it didn't quite work that way.

In the canon of The Universal Law of West Bank Checkpoints, there is a maxim: approach bored soldiers at your peril, or ignore these words and face your doom.

It seemed to be a problem more common to the large "permanent" checkpoints around the countryside, or at the tiny fabricated shacks typically manned by older, reserve-duty men. At these, and specifically the Jerusalem tunnel checkpoint, you could almost guarantee such soldierly gaggles would find a juicy new target in the next car rolling up. And as I cruised up to the inspection lane where such a group had gathered (inspecting photos on each other's cell phones), I knew it wasn't going to go well.

As was the protocol, I pulled up and handed over my passport to a young soldier, who took it, leaned on my car door, and pushed his sunglasses down his nose.

"You are American?" he asked in a heavy accent, looking disbelievingly at the my passport photo (where I looked like a typical American blonde), grinning at the "me" in my passport photo and back again at "me" in my scarf, as if to say, *Whoa! What the hell happened to you!*

Then, he passed the passport over to his friends and they enjoyed a snicker. Typical asshole stuff. Nothing to see here folks.

But it was then that it got really bad. In fact, it was the beginning of what was to be my official entry into the pissing game that we in the "Arab lane" played, by the name of Shittiest Checkpoint Experience Ever. Of course, seasoned travelers back and forth these checkpoints with far worse experiences, but for an amateur player like me, what happened next was bad enough.

Turning to his three companions, the soldier seemed to joke about me in Hebrew as he lifted my CD case out of the passenger seat. Thumbing through it, he again leaned on the open window, "What are these? Do you have Britney Speels? I love Britney Speels," he said, all the while holding up a clipboard with a crudely drawn, but boldly rendered phallus on the back, so that I might see it to its maximum advantage.

Ignoring the artwork, I got out of the car as the soldier instructed, and opened the trunk for inspection; usually the final step before they clear you for passage, but after he inspected it, he still didn't give me back my passport, this time clipping it onto his clipboard, which he still held at an angle, determined that I acknowledge the ridiculous penis. I would not, come hell or high water, or pimple-faced pervert soldier, acknowledge what he was doing.

And that was our stalemate, it seemed. Still, I never got to see how it would have naturally ended because we'd taken up so much time playing his game that a long line of impatient people had formed behind me, prompting the driver next in line to beep his horn and yell from his open window to either turn me back or let me go. And that's when my Shittiest Checkpoint Story gained admissibility.

"You see him?" the soldier asked, pointing his thumb in the direction of my good Samaritan and smiling. "I'm going to make him *pay...* you go," he said, tossing my passport onto my lap and signaling for the man behind me to come forward and presumably learn his lesson for the day in properly submissive behavior.

I drove away, watching the checkpoint shrink in my rear-view mirror. Frustrated, impotent, and feeling slightly dirty, I cried all the way to Jerusalem.

Once in the city, I pulled into a large gas station to fix the eye makeup I'd so carefully applied in the morning, in case Tamar was already at the Promenade. By the time I got there, though, by now more than an hour late, she was nowhere to be found. Tired of being in the car, I decided to sit on a bench and admire the view of the Old City from across the Kidron Valley. Then, I noticed a group of young Palestinian guys (exponentially bolder than their West Bank brothers) sidling up to me, and I decided to wait in my car.

When I finally saw Tamar driving into the parking lot in a shiny new SUV, I was excited and relieved to finally see her but was surprised and a bit disappointed to see that she'd brought her husband along. When he sat in the car after greeting me through the open window, just watching us, as we walked down the main trail, I also got a little suspicious that something was up.

It didn't take long for Tamar to explain that she was worried that maybe I'd changed over the last few months, "You know…with the war." But it wasn't until she pulled out this gem, "Don't you hate Jews, after living so long with them?" that it suddenly became clear that she was afraid of me.

It took a second for my body catch up with the tempest of emotion swirling in my head, but when it did my face heated up. It was a unique feeling, a horrible feeling, but when I tried my best to tell her so—my voice shaking in humiliation and anger, she still went on "…but now that you live there in the Territories…they teach their children to hate us. How can you not hate, now with the war?"

"Tamar!" I interrupted, "do you have any idea what I've been through to even get here today? *I'm* the one passing through checkpoints and running into soldiers in my driveway. *I'm* the one who should be afraid, and if anyone is teaching my kids to hate, it's the soldiers pointing guns at them," I said, my voice shaking.

She looked at me in silence for a moment, as if I were a dense child simply unable to engage in reasonable, adult conversation.

"I don't know, Jenny," she said. "Do you want to go and get a coffee?"

Whatever.

"Sure."

And with that we dropped the conversation, drove to the mall for lattes (Tamar's husband in tow), finished the day with some superficial chitchat and said goodbye.

I never saw her again.

CHAPTER 26

It's All About Who You Know...

Since you cannot do good to all, you are to pay special attention to those who, by the accidents of time, or place, or circumstances, are brought into closer connection with you.

-Augustine of Hippo

I started to feel that time was speeding up once I decided to try to gain access to the off-limits sites on the Temple Mount. But the information I was getting online wasn't exactly encouraging. There were complaints from everyone, from Western archaeology buffs to the faithful who wanted to see the Temple restored to modern-day explorer wannabees (kind of like me) who were angry that they couldn't get access to the Mount. On top of that, the internet buzzed with interest in the underground structures Wilson had described years earlier in his journals.

One of the most worrying articles was from National Geographic magazine, entitled, "Jerusalem's Mysterious Well of Souls," which clearly showed how hard it would be for me to accomplish what I had in mind. In the article, Shimon Gibson, co-author of the work, *Below the Temple Mount in Jerusalem: A Sourcebook on the Cisterns, Subterranean Chambers and Conduits of the Haram Al-Sharif*, said, "Since the nineteenth century, no Westerner has been allowed access to the subterranean chambers on the Temple Mount...I would have liked to disguise myself as a local *Waqf* worker and infiltrate these sites, but I wouldn't want to run the risk of creating an international incident."

International incident?

Still, the idea had merit. After all, I thought, I'm a Westerner, but I'm also a Muslim. For the first time, I thought maybe the combination could work to my advantage.

Ahmad was discouraging when I told him about the idea on Skype. He fell silent, as if embarrassed by my naiveté and confused by my desire to do such a "strange thing."

"They aren't going to let you in," he said. "Don't get your hopes up."

The only problem was, he was right; the aura of suspicion in the Holy Land was as thick as congealed gravy. Add to that the fact that I didn't really know anyone outside of the village who had any connections that could help me with such a daunting goal, and with no connections, professional credits, or expertise to recommend me, I was stuck. Worse, I was a foreigner, and as such, suspicious. I was just Jenny Jones—*Jenny Jones*—could you get more "Western" than that?

I finally realized that the only way I could get near the places I yearned to see would require getting permission from the Islamic authorities, known as the *Waqf*, who controlled the structures on the Mount. In order to do that, I'd have to exemplify what I was—a Westerner and a Muslim—a unique identity I'd neglected to develop and start building some relationships.

I just had to find out with whom.

The tradition of the *Waqf*, or Islamic trust, in the Holy Land, is to ensure that religious sites remain protected and maintained. *Waqf* employees are the "keepers of the holy places," in theory beholden only to God. Of course, under the umbrella of the Occupation, it wasn't that simple.

One of the best things about the Holy Land is that it's a kind of religious beacon for all three of the Abrahamic faiths. Just the thought of the power of the countless prayers spoken either in the land, or aimed at it, seemed to make it almost hum with energy. Unfortunately, many of the most famous holy places have fallen into disrepair because no one can agree on who is responsible for fixing them. After all, whoever does such repairs could indicate that group had a greater claim on them.

Perhaps the best-known example of "holy site hoarding" is the Church of the Holy Sepulchre in the Christian Quarter of the Old City. This church is considered to be the holiest site in the Christian world. The actual building is dark, smoky and mysterious inside, a jarring mix of architectural styles, from Byzantine to Crusader, with a labyrinthine floor plan. One could easily wander around for hours, up tiny stairs, through passageways, even up to the roof, where Ethiopian Orthodox monks claim the space as their own.

In spite of the church's eclectic style, it is a beautiful place—all swinging censers, candlelight, stone, with tiny, dark cavernous chapels opening into soaring cathedral ceilings above. There is an apse through which the Jerusalem sun filters in pale ethereal beams, stretching down to the tomb of Jesus below. There, pilgrims line up one at a time for their moment alone in a tiny tomb hardly large enough for three or four adults to stand in at a time, presided over by a stern Greek Orthodox nun who will abide no nonsense from the faithful (or anyone else for that matter).

Still, the part that was so uniquely Jerusalem was the way the different denominations, represented by their particular priests, monks, nuns and local faithful, fought—literally, and often—to the point of injury with sticks, flying chairs, whatever they could get their hands on. Nobody was allowed to infringe on anyone else's traditional portions of the church—even to clean or repair them. In fact, you can still see a 2008 YouTube video of a melee that erupted when one of the Coptic monks moved his chair from its usual location on the roof a mere twenty centimeters to get a little shade on a hot day. When the Ethiopian monks who control most of the roof, however, noticed, a fistfight between them ensued—hardly an atmosphere that pilgrims from afar expected to find in their holiest of holy places.

It was Peter Shaneb, the Christian Palestinian I'd met before my trip to Jacob's Well who told me, "We can't even agree on who's allowed to sweep the floor of the church. Imagine! The church is filthy in places, and we can't just go in and clean it. You have to get permission from each denomination—Greek Orthodox, Armenians, Roman Catholics, Coptic Orthodox, Ethiopian Orthodox and Syrian Orthodox churches—and that's just not going to happen."

Still, the most famous example of this stalemate (which applies to maintenance, worship times, chapel "ownership," and prayer locations, and a schedule for the times monks may walk through each other's areas), is an old wooden ladder that was placed during the first part of the nineteenth century against the outer wall of the church, where it continues to lean until this day. It serves no purpose, nobody uses it, but it remains immovable, lest someone tip the delicate balance of power over the square inches the small ladder occupies, dusty and gray from the weather.

Of course, the Christians weren't the only Jerusalem residents to fight amongst themselves over their holiest site. Just a short, five-minute walk away was the *Kotel*, or Western Wall, the holiest place in modern Judaism, and there, too, a divide has opened, this time between the Orthodox community (and the Wall's chief rabbi) and those Jews who feel they should be able to either pray with their spouses (men and women are strictly segregated inside of the prayer area at the wall), and a group of religious, Jewish women who call themselves the "Women of the Wall," who feel that they should be able to pray at the Wall in a manner traditionally reserved for men. These women, many of whom consider themselves to be Orthodox as well, believe that it is their religious right to wear prayer shawls, as well as read out loud from the Torah as a group—something only men are presently allowed to do by religious law.

Unfortunately, just as at the church, the disagreement has led to violence, especially between the women and the ultra-Orthodox, who see these activities as an affront to the site, as well as to God.

It only makes sense, then, that when the hoarding goes even farther—jumping religions, as it were— the result would either be self-segregation within the shared locations, or de-facto ownership making them completely off limits to those of other faiths, at sites that used to be shared. Some examples of this kind of exclusive use are Rachel's Tomb, Joseph's Well, the Temple Mount, and countless others across the Holy Land. For tourists and pilgrims, that meant it wasn't enough to have a guidebook in hand to tour the place, and you couldn't just "walk the Bible," even if you wanted to. Still, you could—in all but the most hotly contested sites—at least visit. You just couldn't pray in them—which for many was like getting into Disneyland but not being allowed on the rides.

Because behavior at most of the sites in the Holy Land was "iffy," I had to be very delicate in formulating my requests to the powers that be at the Temple Mount. But first, I had to find out who those powers were. By then, I knew that the Temple Mount had a group of Islamic authorities in charge, called the *Waqf*

However, I didn't know whom to approach, nor had I figured out exactly what I was going to say when I did have a chance. After all, I didn't want to blow it by just breezing in to ask (in my baby Arabic) to see their secret chambers-n-stuff. Because of this, I decided to start small, at one of the scariest and most dangerous places in the West Bank: Hebron's Old City.

Hebron's Tomb of the Patriarchs, or as Palestinians called it, "The Mosque of Abraham," the reported burial site of Abraham and his wife, Sarah, is one of the hottest of hot spots in the region. It is literally divided between the Jewish and Palestinian communities with a harshness found nowhere else in the country, and that's without even considering the neighborhood it's in.

The city's once-thriving old city center is now a ghost town. Its once-bustling shops and produce market closed when the crowds stopped coming, after the settlement and the constant presence of the military. Even those who tried to stay had their shop doors welded shut by the military or by the settlers, themselves. Now the only way to get there from the "Palestinian side" of the city was to walk through a series of fenced corrals snaking through checkpoints and blocks of eerily deserted walkways. These were covered over with chain link to shield pedestrians from the garbage deliberately thrown on them from the settlers above.

The sanctuary itself, built by Herod the Great, resembles an immense rectangular stone box, without visible windows or much detail on the outside. However, inside it's beautiful. There are tapestry-covered cenotaphs, chandeliers, and hand painted arches and vaults. Still, the building shows its age, and its tragic history fairly seeps through the bullet-marked walls. Back in 1994, one of the area's settlers—a physician—entered the mosque during morning prayers and shot and killed twenty-nine worshippers, wounding more than a hundred as they sat in prayer. Now, more than eighteen years after the attack, the tension remains, and soldiers and security are everywhere, often outnumbering visitors.

The shrine itself is divided between the Jewish and Palestinian communities in an uneasy "temporary status agreement." Eighty-one percent of the structure is under control of the Muslim authorities, or *Waqf*, and the remaining under the Jewish community. However, the Israeli military has surrounded the structure and the neighboring streets with a series of pedestrian checkpoints, which means that they have the final decision over who gets in and when—just like at the Temple Mount.

After I entered the Mosque I headed for the guard office, a tall, narrow room made entirely of stone pierced by a large, recessed window that showed the immense thickness of the walls, and explained to the two men present that I would like to learn about their work at the *Waqf*. "So, what's it like taking care of such an important place?" I asked, addressing the small gathering of guards who'd congregated after word spread that someone wanted to learn more about them.

"Well," said one (a dead ringer for Rod Stewart), "it is very difficult… You won't use my name, will you?"

"I don't have to if that's what you prefer," I answered, closing my notebook and placing it on my lap to reassure him.

"It is very difficult, you know…The Jews give us a very hard time, and it is difficult for us to even come to work some days."

"Yes, and the checkpoints are very difficult," said another, the youngest, baby-faced and earnest-looking, sitting at the top of several stone steps leading down to the room's floor.

"Okay, but do you feel proud of the work you are doing here?" I asked, desperate to prevent the conversation from turning into a lament against the Occupation. "I mean, you are taking care of a holy place that people around the world love. Do you feel proud of that?"

"No," said Rod. "Take for instance, this guy here," he said, jerking his thumb in the direction of Babyface. "He has been working here for a year, and he still hasn't been paid. The 'big' people don't care about us and they don't respect us. You know what? When people in the government come here, they don't even greet us. They treat us like garbage, and they pay us almost nothing."

"And how did you guys happen to work here?"

At that, the men gave a list of the names of several old Hebron families that were historically charged with maintaining the site—and whose descendants (as most of the guards were) continue the tradition today. Then, warming up to the topic over a pot of tea and some cigarettes, they all proceeded to complain about the haughtiness of their superiors and the government officials who paid their meager salaries.

Taking this opportunity, I asked for and was given the name and contact information of their superior, so I could talk to him, hoping I could figure out who I needed to approach about my hopes for a Temple Mount visit.

At this point, I was excited, feeling that I'd taken a small step toward my goal, and I thanked the men for their time and their tea, wishing them good luck in the future. Before I left, however, I did ask them to show me the old access tunnel to the caves below the shrine. Here, legend said, death or blindness awaited anyone so bold as to disturb *Sitna Sarah*, "Lady Sarah" in her grave. It was hidden under the prayer carpets and now cemented over, lest the faithful from the synagogue next door try to break into the cave as they had in the past, seeking a connection with the remains of their ancestors. This would, of course, have been in violation of Islamic sensibilities, which prohibit "disturbing the dead."

In the end, it was a satisfying day. I had negotiated the neighborhood and the checkpoints, my Arabic had stood up pretty well, and I'd gotten the all-important *Waqf* contact information to start my journey toward the Mount. In fact, I felt pretty darn proud of myself.

All that changed the moment I logged onto the Internet that evening, did a new search, and discovered that the *Waqf* governing the rest of the Holy Land's Islamic sites was a different entity entirely from the one on the Temple Mount (which, strangely enough, turned out to be under the authority of the Jordanian government as a legacy of the 1967 War, not the Palestinian Authority as I had supposed). It meant the day's "connection" wouldn't help me at all.

Ah, well, back to square one.

I had always passed Hebron University on my way to work, and I often wondered what it was like inside its walled campus, but I'd never had had a chance to stop in. One day, though, it occurred to me as I stopped at the main traffic light near the campus, students strolling by in tight little single-sex groups, that a job at *the* Islamic university in the West Bank might give me the credibility I need to make some real connections. There were just two problems: I only had a Bachelor's degree, which made me under-qualified to teach there, and I had a nasty public-speaking phobia—a bit of a problem for an aspiring university instructor.

Sure, I had taught at the software company, but there my only "audience" was a handful of software engineers sitting around a conference table. Still, the idea somehow stuck in my mind and I decided to apply anyway, let them consider my qualifications (or lack thereof), and worry about my public speaking terrors another day.

Less than a week later, I received an email from the Vice President of the University, Dr. Atawneh. It just so happened they had a vacancy!

When I arrived for my meeting with Dr. Atawneh, I strolled through the large, domed gate straight into a student demonstration in the courtyard. It appeared to be something straight out of a political cartoon. It was an impressive tableau—all satin headbands, flags and raised fists—only without any of the real heat you'd see in the street, which I confirmed as I made my way through the crowd toward the administration building. These students just smelled too good, smiled a little too much, and somehow seemed too shiny to be fierce. It was my first exposure to the university's student culture—intense, romantic, perfectly angst-ridden, and always impeccably dressed.

I entered the administration building, a modern cement structure at the front of the university, and introduced myself to the receptionist, whose jaw dropped slightly as I spoke to her in my accent. It was a common reaction, especially when I approached people suddenly, before they had a chance to check me out, and they realized the sounds coming out of my mouth were not as expected. It was as if I'd lifted a mask and said, "Boo!"

After recovering from her momentary confusion, the receptionist escorted me to Dr. Atawneh's office.

"Welcome, Jennifer!" said Dr. Atawneh as he rose and came toward me, smiling broadly. "What's your policy on shaking hands?" he said, referring to the widespread Muslim belief that hand shaking between the sexes is strictly forbidden.

"If someone offers, I shake; otherwise, I don't shake hands," I replied.

"Excellent policy, Jennifer," he laughed, gesturing for me to have a seat across from him at his desk.

"Well," he started, "I think we can probably help each other, but it will be up to the heads of the English Department to determine your suitability to teach a class or two. How does that sound?"

Within days, I was scheduled for an interview, first by the dean of the English Department, middle-aged and exuding a peculiar old-school ladies-man vibe, and with three other professors, who grilled me on teaching theory, writing styles, and the methods I used in my other teaching job.

Doing my best to feign confidence, I struggled to recall the nebulous memory of a distant, solitary undergraduate class on education. I focused on *not* mentioning my use of YouTube as curriculum, and did my best to answer most of their questions with a semblance of good sense.

In all truth, it was a moment far removed from my timid-housewife days back home, and it actually felt good.

The next day, I got a call from the Dean, himself, offering me an open class section in advanced English composition, and I was in!

CHAPTER 27

Pretty Birds

I'm not denyin' the women are foolish:
God Almighty made 'em to match the men.

-GEORGE ELIOT

My mother-in-law's general dubiousness about my work in Hebron meant I was very nervous to tell the family that I was going to be adding the class at the university to my schedule. Happily, I was surprised to see that she actually seemed impressed when I told her that I was going to be a "real teacher." Palestinians are obsessive about education, and even though both she and my father-in-law are illiterate (forced to sign legal documents with a thumbprint like many of the older generation), she uses all her powers of grandmotherly guilt to push the family's kids to cutthroat competition for the highest grades in the village.

So when I found out from Asya that she'd been bragging around Safa about her "son's wife, the university teacher," I couldn't help but feel a sense of satisfaction. If my job at the university could accomplish that miracle, maybe it was a good sign.

When I showed up for my first class a few weeks later, located four floors above the cafeteria in one of the newer buildings on campus, I was dressed in the unofficial uniform of the university: a long trench-coat like *jilbab*—a new one in the season's ultra-fashionable corduroy, and a carefully wrapped rectangular scarf.

At first, nobody seemed to notice me as they assembled in the large room, perhaps assuming that I was just another student, until I plopped down my laptop on the podium and started talking—in English. Jaws dropped and the class quieted to a shocked attention. There was no question that this class wouldn't be what the students expected.

Most of the students in the university, somewhere around seventy-three percent, were female, but in my class I would have placed it closer to ninety percent. Like me, they all wore Islamic dress. But that was where the similarity ended.

Whereas I've struggled for years to arrange my scarf in a way that does not make me resemble a Russian nesting doll, the Hebron students seemed to have elevated Islamic style to a whole other plane of awesome-ness, wearing scarves wrapped and folded like origami, with matching makeup, shoes and bags in hues bright as tropical birds. According to the dean, most of the girls were majoring in marriage, an idea that I couldn't readily dismiss—especially since the majority of them showed up to writing class without pens or paper. Even the few male students were all polished and shiny, wearing pointy dress shoes, polyester pants and gelled coifs reminiscent of *Saturday Night Fever*. It was certainly a far cry from the flip-flops and sweats from my college days, and I felt posi-tively frumpy in comparison.

Still, the first class began well, and once the students recovered from their initial shock at my rapid-fire English, they seemed to be quite interested.

I was most pleased that my worst fears—that I would stammer ner-vously, or forget what to talk about—seemed to float away on the little white puffs of my words in the unheated building. *This might be easier than I thought.*

Sadly, Murphy's Law is in effect in the Holy Land, too, and my bright idea of having the class go around and introduce themselves (after all, advanced composition is a bit like a Writing 101 class back home) hit the brakes on my dreams of being Awesome Teacher of the Year.

"And you…what's your name," I asked, addressing one of the four male students seated at the rear of the room.

"Mahmood."

"Okay, Mahmood, tell us about yourself and what you hope to learn in this class," I said, looking down at my class list, ready to pencil in his response.

"I don't want to talk," he grumbled, staring me down like a stubborn toddler.

Confused, I was about to move on to someone else when another student, a tiny girl wearing a peacock-colored pashmina hijab and seated in the front row, interjected, "It's common for the boys not to talk much in class."

Now, I'm sure the girl (who became one of my top students) wanted to help by acquainting the new teacher with the lay of the land, perhaps diffusing the sudden tension that everyone in the room could plainly feel. But there was just *something* about the boy's offended air, as if I had breached some unspoken rule against calling on the boys that raised my hackles.

Bullshit, I thought, this is an advanced university class—and it was *my* class. If it had been a few months earlier, I probably would have let it slide, but not anymore. *This little shit is going to learn a lesson,* I thought. So, after giving him one final chance to participate (which he again refused), I kicked him out of the class and spent the rest of the period mediating an argument between the rival Hamas and Palestinian Authority affiliated students, giving my first lesson in "keeping it on the page" instead of arguing.

After class, I decided to walk over to the dean's office to make sure Mr. Non-Talker would be permanently removed from my section. It was something I found particularly important to do, given that he had refused to leave the room until I threatened to call security. *That* I wouldn't let slide!

I'm not sure what I expected—acknowledgment of the problem, maybe disciplinary action (after all, I don't remember a particularly high tolerance for student disrespect in the universities I'd attended). However, when I sat across from the dean in his office and explained the problem, all I got was a blank stare, a cloud of cigarette smoke, and a smile.

Leaning back, he finally offered, "Well, it's a writing class. Is it really necessary that he *speak*?"

After taking a second to process the Dean's question, I managed to stammer out that, yes, I did prefer that my students speak during class. At this, the Dean laughed, shook his head, and told me that they routinely allowed male students to change class sections if they were outnumbered by their female peers.

It was an idea that left me literally speechless. After all, how many times have female students been outnumbered by men, especially in technical fields? This was ridiculous. There was no way I was going to play that game. Still, I thought, maybe I was missing something, perhaps some kind of sexist favoritism, a nod to male pride. This isn't my culture, I thought. Maybe I just didn't get it.

"Oh, and Jennifer," the dean added, "Here is the key to your office. It's in the new building, and I think you'll like it. It is a bit small, though," he continued. "But your body is nice and slim…It should fit just fine."

Nice.

Exhausted and more than a little creeped out, I quickly took my leave of the Dean and hurried over to the administration building to meet Beth in Public Relations. She was the only other American at the university, and I'd met her that first day in Dr. Atawneh's office. She was a sweet American student studying Arabic and Hebrew in the Holy Land, but she'd never been to downtown Hebron. So I offered to take her.

What I didn't know at the time was that the night we went would be when Hebron's settlers decided to torch the city, and by the time we got to downtown we'd found ourselves in a melee—leaping flames, exploding percussion grenades, and intermittent gunfire. Together, we walked to the edge of the downtown market, and blinking through the remnants of tear-gas clouds, watched the neighborhood burn, hoping it wasn't an omen of worse things to come.

CHAPTER 28

Murder in Bat Ayin

Terrorism doesn't just blow up buildings; it blasts every other issue off the political map. The spectre of terrorism—real and exaggerated—has become a shield of impunity, protecting governments around the world from scrutiny for their human rights abuses.

-Naomi Klein

My kids had mastered the art of using my newfound working-mother guilt to their advantage, and this time they talked me into taking them to Solomon's Pools again. The April weather was warm and clear, and I decided to give them a rare pizza picnic (take-out from a Bethlehem restaurant called Milano's) right across the road from the pools on a clean-looking platform in the abandoned, crumbling visitors center.

After they finished, the kids ran straight over to the pools, especially the largest one that they called "the slide" (where they all tore out the bottom of their pants against the rough plastered chute). As I busied myself packing up the mess and throwing away the garbage, though, I looked up to a balcony above me and saw what appeared to be the figure of a man, hurriedly darting out of sight. Realizing that we were being watched and possibly followed was enough for me to hurry up, gather the kids and head back to the village.

Once we neared the military tower at the mouth of the village road, we could see that a checkpoint had been erected and that a large, steel gate had been locked shut across the road. Not sure what to do, I parked the car on the edge of the road and approached the three soldiers at the checkpoint, two of whom raised their rifles to my chest. Addressing them in English (as I'd learned was usually the best move in uncertain situations with the Israeli military), I asked them why the road was closed.

"Go ask your friends. They will tell you," answered a middle-aged soldier.

My friends. What the hell was he talking about? Ignoring the remark, I continued, "Well, how can we get through? I have to get my kids home."

"The road is closed, and the town is a closed military zone. You go...." He said, turning his face from me and walking away as if I were too low to deserve a full sentence. His job was to close, not advise, whether there were kids in the car or not. I would have to find another way to get back to the village and find out what was going on.

I turned the car around and decided to try for home via an unpaved back road that was generally off the military patrol grid. I still didn't know the details of the closure, so I hoped the soldiers hadn't closed the back entrances, too. So with no other choice, I headed to the town of Halhoul, near Hebron, to start the slow, bumpy ride to the village.

Two hours later we were finally back home in Safa. There we were met with very unwelcome news: the village was closed because someone in Safa had infiltrated a neighboring Jewish settlement, called Bat Ayin, and murdered a thirteen-year-old boy with an ax.

Everybody was trying to guess who could have killed the child, and everybody started whispering their suspicions. So far, though, nobody I knew seemed to have any real ideas, which was surprising. After all, one thing I knew about Safa was that *nobody* in the village could keep a secret.

Without any information about the culprit, then, we all turned to mutual rumination, trying to make personal, moral sense of the crime. Then, arguments started to break out, and some—mostly young men— said that if the reports were true that one boy was killed and another critically injured when a young male attacked them with a pick ax on the lawn of one of the settlement buildings—then it was justified because of Bat Ayin's history of attacks against the village.

Many others, though—most of them, parents (this parent included) —argued that kids, of all people, are off limits. *No matter what.*

It was a strange feeling that there might be a killer—an ax killer— in our midst here in small Safa, where basically everyone was related to everyone else by blood or marriage. *Somebody* had to know who he was—and that was exactly why the military decided to close the village. Squeeze us all and somebody will talk.

It's a logical theory unless you happened to be one of the unlucky residents who didn't know squat. Then, you were going down with the rest, baby. We could only hunker down and wait. Problem was, there was another layer to the situation that cast a dark cloud over us all, and this layer was much more insidious.

Everyone in Safa knew that they would eventually find the killer by closing off the village, searching and interrogating. That was going to be painful, yes. But the really dark cloud in all of this was the coming retribution from the settlement. It was only a matter of time, and if the village was closed and none of us could escape, we were going to be sitting ducks.

Although no one seemed to know who had committed this latest crime, everyone knew some kind of reprisal would be coming against Safa. That was just how it worked between settler communities and Palestinian villages—especially when the settlement was one like Bat Ayin.

The issue of settlements (communities built within occupied territory) is one of the main sticking points of the Israeli-Palestinian conflict. According to international law, they are illegal, yet they not only remain throughout the West Bank, East Jerusalem, and the Golan Heights, but they are growing, both in population, land expansion, and in the number of new outposts across the countryside.

As for the settlers themselves, I couldn't help but find them oddly fascinating. Most of the settlements were there for religious, nationalistic, or even financial reasons, and they built huge, modern, fenced communities that stood in sharp contrast to the Palestinian villages alongside them. These settlements even had lawns—lawns!—when most Palestinian villages were forced to ration the water they used for similarly frivolous things—like drinking.

Bat Ayin was another story altogether.

The settlement was considered so hard-core, it didn't even need a fence. In fact, the settlers were famous for their assertion that "our fence is as far as we can shoot." My father-in-law was unfortunate enough to confirm this when he unwittingly entered into that area while out grazing his sheep one day. Still, he was lucky. All he lost were a few hours, hunkered belly-down in the rocks, along with one lost lamb—shot straight through its neck by the settlers.

Unfortunately, the neighborly relations between the two communities had claimed much more than that in sacrifice over the years, including a 2002 attempt by a group of Bat Ayin residents to bomb a girls' elementary school in East Jerusalem, and several tit-for-tat attacks and murders that left the two communities at dangerous odds.

Although we still didn't know who'd done the crime, everyone knew that a reprisal was coming against Safa. After all, collective punishment was standard operating procedure in the West Bank, and the soldiers weren't even shy to say it (despite the awkward fact that collective punishment is against international law).

One soldier, blessed with amazingly glossy, blond *peyos* pushed back under his helmet straps, expressed the "logic" perfectly to me at a checkpoint a few weeks before when someone threw a stone at their concrete guard tower: "If one of you throws rocks at us, we close your town…If you don't like it, tell your kids not to throw stones."

My kids?

"My kids are right here in the back seat," I said, pointing my thumb at the three of them.

I never got the reaction I was looking for.

Still, Safa had it easy compared to the main towns along the highway, where rocks and Molotov cocktails were more common. But even as far away as we were, we'd lost power and been "closed" (literally, a giant iron gate was permanently installed so it could be opened and locked at will by the military) because of boys throwing stones or Molotovs at passing convoys in a neighboring town.

This was based on a bizarre belief that "the others" (us) were a living, breathing entity, as if all every Palestinian within any given radius not only knew, but also *controlled* each other. That was the root of the problem and is similar to the thinking of a suicide bomber choosing to push the button in public, next to a stroller. After all, "they" are The Enemy, so no further thought is required. Now it was a notion that filled me with unspeakable dread.

An uneasy day passed until a report finally came from the neighboring town's municipality that an attack was imminent, generating a wave of hysteria. For literally the first time in their lives, the village children were told to beware of strangers and were terrified. I didn't let my kids play outside at all.

The army came in late the next night, along with a test attack by the Bat Ayin settlers. Flares lit up the sky and the house shook from percussion grenades and helicopters, leaving us to stay holed up inside our homes, talking to each other by cell phone.

By morning, the army had completely taken over the streets, broken into homes and made arrests. But in the light of day, the residents seemed to be braver, running between the houses, getting updates and exchanging supplies until dusk, when the activity again quieted.

But when darkness came and the army began patrolling again, the soldiers seemed to have something new in store. Again and again, they blared a message from their vehicles into the night: Every man and boy over the age of twelve must surrender themselves at the village crossroads.

My son Ibrahim was twelve-and-a-half.

CHAPTER 29

Escape

*When I see how we treat one another; the war, the crime,
the inhumanity...I wonder a million years ago whether we
crawled out of the slime or were asked to leave.*

-MILT ABEL

"All men and boys over twelve must report to the bottom of the
road. Anyone not following orders will be shot."

My fourteen-year-old niece, Manar, was with me in the dark
kitchen, straining to understand the announcement, which was garbled
by the night wind, percussion grenades, and the speaker's accent.

"...Anyone not following orders will be shot."

It was the last part of the order that took me so long to understand.
Finally, with a sharp pain that passed from my forehead to my gut, the
words sank in. Manar must have come to the understanding at the same
moment because her voice rose to a high-pitched shriek. "Oh, my God,
Jenny! They're going to take Ibrahim!"

Trying hard not to panic, I rested my head against the window frame,
franticly thinking over my options. I peered again over the window's
casement. Several Israeli Army Jeeps and armored personnel carriers
cruised slowly up the road, their spinning yellow lights casting long
shadows behind men walking the back orchard.

There was no way I was sending my son down there.

Ibrahim was twelve, but could easily pass for fifteen or older. *God, why did he have to be so cursedly tall?!* For the first time, I actually wished my son was small for his age, like his cousins. Their moms were probably keeping them home, safe where they belonged. *I can hide him…maybe behind the big boiler on the roof.* But Ibrahim couldn't even keep himself quiet for a game of hide and seek with his sister. Besides, I couldn't bear the thought of him crouching up there, all alone. In my mind's eye I saw boots thumping up the stairs. All it would take was one noise, one spooked soldier with a nervous trigger finger, and that would be it.

No, it was far too risky. But then again, so was handing him over to the soldiers. Bat Ayin was arguably the most radical settlement in the entire West Bank. They believed that whoever had killed the child in their settlement came from Safa, and they had already taken steps to punish us.

"Blame the killer that you don't have milk for your children," one soldier said.

What's more, since Bat Ayin was infamous for its motto, "For every one of us injured, three of them dead," I couldn't count on them having scruples against hurting or killing one of our kids. True, the army was supposed to hold themselves to a different standard—but then again, if they were willing to cut off our access to food and milk for the village kids and babies, would they protect our boys from the settlers, or would they simply hand them over?

I'd seen the army back the settlers too many times, so I made my decision: we were going to make a run for it.

Hurrying downstairs, Manar woke the kids and helped them change out of their pajamas. She gave them a quick explanation about needing to get away from tear gas and percussion grenades, which were increasing, though still distant. I knew there was no way the kids had heard or understood the order from the Israeli soldiers, and decided it was better to keep it that way—especially for Ibrahim's sake.

I moved quickly, grabbing our passports, some money, and a credit card. I had no idea where we would go, but I didn't care. The only thing that mattered was getting Ibrahim out of Safa.

Within five minutes I was backing the car out of the garage and down the dark driveway. Although the windows were closed, I could still feel the telltale burn of tear gas in the back of my throat, and I realized I'd forgotten to close the vents in the car. I quickly did so and silently prayed the wind would blow most of the gas past the car on our way out of the village.

The kids were uncharacteristically quiet as I turned the car onto the unpaved road in front of the house. They were silenced by the sudden flash-boom! of the grenades and the eerie sight of the army's spotlights, shooting through the fog like fat laser beams. Only Karim spoke—all wide-eyed in his car seat—exclaiming, "Scare my belly!" with each new explosion we heard.

The short road was so rocky and rutted that it took more than ten minutes at a bouncing crawl to finally reach the paved road that led to Beit Ommar. Once there, I slowly continued the remaining fifty feet to the crest of the small hill that unofficially marked the boundary of the village. Seeing nothing on the other side, I turned to Manar in the passenger seat, and smiled. We'd made it!

As we coasted down the hill and away from Safa, I started to think about where to go next, entertaining visions of a cozy, safe hotel room in nearby Bethlehem. Rounding the corner, however, I faced a sight so terrifying that I slammed on my breaks, forgetting the clutch, and stopped in a shuddering stall that marked the end of my reverie.

You don't just leave town in the middle of a siege. An earthen barrier had been bulldozed across the road, completely eliminating any possibility of escape. Worse, though, were the four armored personnel carriers sitting directly in front of us—the only car on the road—their spotlights trained on my windshield.

Waqif! "Halt!" Even with the windows up, I could hear the order. I steadied my hand enough to roll down the window a crack, terrified I would miss some crucial command. I was afraid to restart the car, afraid to approach further, and just as afraid to try turning around. So I sat motionless, cursing my impulsive decision to leave.

I waited, hoping my yellow plates would reassure them enough not to shoot at us—or at least give them pause. Finally a flashlight signaled us to approach the long earthen berm in front of the vehicles, and I restarted the car, slowly creeping forward to where a lone soldier had emerged onto the road.

Although I was accustomed to having guns pointed my way at the omnipresent checkpoints dotting the West Bank, there was something about the way this soldier paused, pointing his gun at each one of us, individually, that made my skin prickle. The look on his face was so utterly devoid of emotion, yet robotically fierce at the same time, it was the scariest encounter I'd ever had with another human being.

I knew, *knew*, that he would shoot us all if I made one wrong move, so I sat completely still; I'm not even sure I remembered to breathe.

A long pause later, the soldier backed stiffly away without a word. I slowly turned the car around and started back to Safa.

No. There would be no escape.

We waited until the garage door closed behind us before we felt it was safe to get out of the car. Since Karim had fallen asleep, I carried him back inside and lay him in his bed. I turned on the cartoon channel for Ibrahim and Amani, and called Manar into the bedroom to talk.

"This is what we're going to do," I said, giving her a look as confident as I could muster. "I'm taking Ibrahim outside to the drop-off point at the bottom of the street. I want you to stay here with Karim and Amani."

The look on her face was one of defeat. I saw that she, too, knew we had no choices left.

"Everything's going to be fine." I continued. "I'll just have to talk the soldiers out of keeping him. But listen, don't say anything to Ibrahim, and don't cry. I don't want to scare him. Do you understand?"

Manar nodded and followed me back into the family room, where she sat on the couch next to Amani and Ibrahim, whose faces were illuminated by the flickering images of Tom and Jerry.

"Ibrahim, come here for a minute," I said, motioning my son into the entryway. *Why did he have to be so tall?*

"Listen, honey. You and I are going to go down and talk to the soldiers for a few minutes, and I need you to be very brave, okay?"

"But why?" he asked, "Just us?"

I felt sick. I didn't want to scare him, but I didn't want to lie to him either. Still, I'd kept him in the dark about the announcement and I couldn't bring myself to tell him the full truth now. It was the only thing I could control, a meager protection I wanted to continue for as long as possible.

"You're the man of the house, Ibrahim," I said. "And the soldiers want to talk to the leaders of each family. That's you and me, right?"

"Oh, okay, Mom," he said, clearly proud of his big boy role.

"Just be brave, do what they say, and everything will be fine." I added, patting his back, hoping he didn't notice the catch in my throat.

"I'm not scared, Mom."

"Good, honey." I turned away and grabbed him a sweatshirt from the closet, quickly wiping the tears from my eyes before they had a chance to fall.

"Let's go."

Hand in hand, we walked away from the house and then turned down the road toward the announced drop-off point. My unsuccessful escape plan had consumed so much time that we were noticeably late responding to the order. I didn't want to startle anyone with our approach, so I joked with Ibrahim in an intentionally loud voice—hoping to put our foreign status on conspicuous display at the same time.

It wasn't long before the sound of crackling walkie-talkies told me we were getting close, and as we neared the dark intersection I could barely make out an eerily silent mass of boys and men crouching with their hands on their heads by the side of the road. Aside from the broken, electronic bursts of Hebrew, the only other sound was the village's power transformers above us, arcing in the fog as if in a cheap production of Frankenstein. Their tiny zigzags of light emanated with each buzzing pulse, as if the army had somehow conspired with the elements to make the moment as terrifying as possible.

As we approached, a flashlight shone in our faces and a voice barked in hard Arabic, "Leave the boy and go."

Putting my arm around Ibrahim's shoulders, I pulled him to me, answering the flashlight in clear, loud English. "I'm sorry, but I can't leave him with you. He doesn't speak Hebrew or Arabic, so he can't stay here."

A pause, and some murmuring in Hebrew, then the beam of the flashlight lowered. A tall soldier that I took for the unit commander stepped toward me out of the gloom.

"You'll do what we tell you to do," he said firmly.

A hot flash of hate surged through me, and I forced my face into a fierce, rigid smile. I answered again in purposely obtuse English, trying to look stupid and authoritative at the same time. "Well, see, he's only twelve. And you know you aren't allowed to hold children. And like I said, he can't understand Arabic. If you want to keep him, I'll have to stay, too."

"Give me your ID!" the man snapped. As I stepped forward to obey his order, Khalid emerged out of the crowd of prisoners, trying to intervene. As one, the entire unit raised their rifles, yelling at Khalid to get back. Next to me, I could feel Ibrahim starting to shake.

I knew Khalid was risking his life, and I also knew I might not win this. But once again, I plastered a smile on my face and repeated in English "American" as many times as possible, as much to distract the soldiers from Khalid as to support my case.

Obviously flustered, the commander stepped closer to me, flanked by two other soldiers who looked like they were still in high school. Pushing his glasses up the bridge of his nose, the commander snatched the passports out of my hand, flipping too quickly through the documents to actually read the information.

I'm sure I was the last thing he'd expected to see that night—a pesky foreigner in the middle of West Bank nowhere—witness to an illegal roundup that was probably his idea, and I was counting on the possibility that the commander might decide that keeping Ibrahim would be more trouble than it was worth. After all, I'd seen it before at checkpoints, a sudden change in behavior once the soldiers realized I wasn't a Palestinian, a kind of frustrated embarrassment occasionally mixed with an honest streak of compassion.

A long moment passed while the commander considered what to do, stepping away to confer with his soldiers. We waited, Ibrahim focusing his attention fixed on his uncle, and me, trying to maintain a confident pose with my arm still clamped hard around my son's shoulders.

Finally, the commander handed our passports to one of the young soldiers. The soldier stepped forward, returned the documents to me, and with a wave of his hand dismissed us with a quick, clipped, "Take him and go!"

We walked away, leaving Khalid and the rest of the village's boys and men to fade back into the dark, squatting with their hands on their heads just as we found them. It wasn't the first time I felt guilty for using my American "privilege," but it was by far the worst. I couldn't—no, I *wouldn't*—risk my child to make a point, but I also couldn't stop thinking about the other children, watching us walk away by virtue of that one magic word: American.

When the soldiers came to search the house that night, I'd already been watching from the top of the front tower, bundled up in a blanket and perched on a plastic chair for more than two hours. I watched them approach, banging their rifle butts on the garage door. *Iftah al Bab!* "Open the door!"

By the time I made it all the way down the three flights of stairs, the kids were awake, startled by the loud banging. I opened the garage and five soldiers entered, blinking in the sudden light and ordering us to leave the house while they searched.

This was the last straw in an already too long night for Karim, who started crying (loudly) as I carried him out into the night air. It was a weird feeling, knowing that soldiers were inside my bedroom, going through my drawers, bathroom, toys. However, as long as I had the kids safely by my side, nothing else mattered.

When the soldiers emerged from the house, one of them paused to pick up a toy gun from the garage floor. He started to laugh as he walked over to Karim, patted him on the back, and said, "Don't cry, little man!" The soldier then handed the gun to Ibrahim, turned and wished us a "pleasant night" before disappearing into the darkness.

Morning came with news that Safa's prisoners had been freed, with only a few taken away for questioning—thankfully, none of them children. The army was still at the crossroads, as well as at a half-dozen other locations inside the village, but we were free to move between the houses.

Safa remained closed, however. The only access was a single road that snaked through the settlement. We all watched as a black, shiny Suburban that belonged to one of the few embedded news crews crept slowly down the hill from the settlement. The SUV stood out in contrast to the military vehicles and Safa's few dusty, dilapidated cars. Once it entered Safa, someone in the Suburban rolled down the black-tinted (probably, bulletproof) windows just long enough to say they were looking for an English-speaking person to interview. Of course, the village kids, who took to running alongside the beautiful foreigner's car, quickly directed them to the only American in Safa—me.

I don't know, maybe it was the stress of the previous night finally catching up to me, but that reporter, all spiffy and beautiful, emerging from the car and typing on her Blackberry, rubbed me the wrong way. Or maybe last night had nothing to do with it. Maybe she irked me because, as she placed the phone in her back pocket, she walked down my drive and passed right by me, obviously looking for someone more "American" to talk to. Oh, and did I mention that she was flanked by three huge bodyguards in mirrored sunglasses?

"Can I help you with something?" I asked the woman.

"Oh!" She seemed startled by my English as she tossed her hair. "Yes, can you tell me what's been happening here?"

"Well, that depends…" I answered, eyeing the three men standing a few feet behind her, hands clasped and feet apart in that universally recognized, tough guy pose. "Who are you?"

"I am with an American news organization," she said. "We want to hear about what's going on here…"

"Which news organization?" I asked.

Let's just say that when I heard her answer, delivered with an obvious pride that defied all explanation, I shooed her biased, embedded ass and her "protection" off my property like a redneck with a shotgun. I admit, I might have exuded more than a smidge of misplaced aggression, but a few choice words and the summoning of the neighbors was all it took to send that shiny Suburban away in a hail of dust and gravel, ostensibly to find someone far more fair, and definitely more balanced to interview.

By late afternoon, the military was completely gone, leaving the village in a strangely calm state. Word passed between the families that nobody in Safa had been arrested, and we began to doubt that the killer came from our tiny village at all.

CHAPTER 30

Safety in Numbers

Fear can make a donkey attack a lion.

-ARAB PROVERB

Over the next few days, things seemed to calm down enough that I began to think life in Safa might return to normal. Although I'd begun to seriously consider leaving early, there wasn't anything I could do quickly because the village remained closed. In spite of this, I felt almost relaxed, somehow, as if the fear and relief I had felt the night of the raid had lulled me into a feeling that the worst was over—and honestly, I felt a little numb after the experience. Still, I was about to come around real quick.

It was a beautiful, sunny April day on the morning of the attack, and I awoke to loud pounding on the garage doors. Still in my pajamas, I ran to the garage, thinking it was Manar or my mother-in-law, but as soon as I saw the number of feet that appeared behind the rising door, I knew something was horribly wrong. Reflexively running for my prayer scarf to cover my pajamas, I heard the first group of people come in the house, talking in tones tinged with hysteria. When I came back from my room, I saw that more people, some of whom I'd never met, were coming in with their young children, asking to take shelter in our safety room, which was specially outfitted with thick concrete walls, steel window covers and a bulletproof door.

That was when the next-door mosque's loudspeaker crackled to life, sending out a young boy's voice through the village air, suddenly laced with whistles, the universal Palestinian warning that meant *soldiers are coming. . .*

Only this time it was going to be much worse.

"Settlers! We are under attack! Safa is under attack, come help us!" It was a distress message carried from the mosque next door to the next one down the valley, and from there to the neighboring villages in a kind of village-to-village Morse-code. It was faster than cell phones, and it was also infinitely more terrifying than the gunfire already echoing across the hills.

Waking the kids, I rushed them into the safety room to join the growing crowd, including Manar and Rawan, who ran in to talk to me in the kitchen. They told me that all of the village men and boys were heading to the edge of the village to try and head off the settlers before they could get in among the houses. At that, the three of us ran up to the roof and looked north toward the ridge between Safa and the Bat Ayin, where plumes of smoke rose against the blue sky.

It was then that I heard a noise similar to the private airplanes I was used to back home (something I never saw in the Holy Land). Looking up, I spotted it, but instead of a Cessna, it was a drone flying directly above me, circling over the house like a vulture.

Now I was *really* scared, and I ran as fast as I could downstairs to seal the door to the safety room, telling Amani not to open it from inside unless she was sure it was me or someone else she knew, scaring her so badly that she jerked the door closed before I could move my hand from the doorjamb, slamming it hard on my fingers.

There was obviously so much adrenaline pumping through my body that I could ignore the new, odd shape—and after a few moments—the pain in my pinky finger, obviously broken just above the middle joint.

Word spread that my house was the place to go, and more people—mostly women and children—continued to stream in, betting that it would be safer to be with the American (after all, most of them had seen how much power my passport had that night at the intersection), even if the safety room was full. Not wanting to keep anyone outside, some of them took up door watch in the garage, ready to shut the steel if they spotted settlers coming.

Not knowing what was going on outside was unbearable, so Manar and I ran upstairs once again, just in time to see a mass of people in white come up over the ridge armed with automatic rifles. Although we couldn't see the "front line" over the ridge, the men and boys seemed to be holding them back for a few minutes with slingshots and stones. It wasn't long before they were running in our direction, though, chased by the settlers. Now, the military had arrived, too—advancing down the road, using live fire, percussion grenades and tear gas.

Soon, what seemed to be the entire male population of Safa was running past the front of my house, followed by a gaggle of journalists wearing blue-helmets and bulletproof vests marked PRESS, furiously snapping photos of the men as they tried to dig in at the orchard across the street for a new volley of stones. Somehow, the settlers seemed to have paused—perhaps put off by the growing cloud of tear gas that was being shot at the villagers. It was drifting now, becoming an effective, if temporary, barrier between the two groups.

The soldiers, however, continued to advance, but were driven into Huda's house by the stone throwers, which they quickly emptied of the remaining family members with a sound bomb and a cloud of tear gas.

Huda was the next person to make for my house, carrying her eight-year-old son, who was overcome by the gas. And now the action was front-row between my driveway and Huda's home, the upper floor of which was quickly being destroyed by the soldiers smashing out windows and screens to shoot at the stone throwers. The stone throwers, oblivious in their fury, were smashing the home's outer stone work, which was falling in huge chunks to the cement walkway below.

Unable to watch her home being destroyed, and traumatized to see it suddenly occupied, Huda ran for her house as the press turned to film her hitting her own face in despair, oblivious to the danger as she made for her back door. Luckily, Manar and I ran out to stop her before she could burst in on the soldiers, and we dragged her back to my house, missing a slipper—which she'd somehow lost as we pulled her back—screaming toward her home, "Shoot me! Shoot me!"

It was then that the soldiers decided to abandon Huda's house for mine, presumably because it was the highest point around and directly above the orchard where the stone-throwers were hiding. In fact, I think it was one of them who sneaked through the field next to my house to come and warn us that the soldiers were at the front door, ready to break in the iron-clad frame.

By then, the press had moved into position in front of the house, snapping pictures of the Israeli unit hunkered down and ready to storm in while Safa's women, children, sick and disabled cowered inside. Realizing that if they came in, we would have nowhere to go but outside into the bullets, the gas, and the settlers, I decided to try to dissuade them before they got in. I ran out, still in my prayer scarf and pajamas, to once again use my "let's be reasonable now" mantra the best that I could—this time on camera.

Later that night, my husband watched the evening news and saw a film clip of me trying to persuade the soldiers to kindly remove their jack from my front door—which, amazingly, they did. He called that night, demanding I return to Seattle with the kids.

Part Five

The Road to Jerusalem

CHAPTER 31

Pressing On...

Constant exposure to dangers will breed contempt for them.

-Marcus Annaeus Seneca

T he dust settled, and Safa swept up from the attack and assessed the damage. In all, it had been relatively light. Two people had been critically wounded by gunfire, and others were gone, hauled away to prison for questioning, including a mentally disabled nephew and his brother, who were beaten with an iron bar on the way to detention.

Then, there was the property damage: smashed windows, stolen property (cell phones were particularly popular with sticky fingered soldiers), and some fire damage to trees and fields. All of the windows, screens, and stone work were destroyed on the second floor of Huda's home (which had taken them more than five years to build on the family's meager incomes).

The most interesting bit of information, though, was that the killer had reportedly been found—an eighteen-year-old boy from a house down the road who reportedly had decided that he would simply walk into the settlement and kill the first person he could in revenge for a beating endured by a young relative months before.

I was surprised by how fast the kids—mine and everyone else's—rebounded after the violence ended, or at least seemed to. The only lasting signs of trauma were the near constant "invasion" games that dominated the play time of virtually every child in the village, boys and girls, alike.

Although I seriously considered leaving, the news that the killer had been found made me reconsider, and although Ahmad wasn't exactly happy with the decision, he didn't force the issue. In fact, I was surprised when he told me that he respected my decision, adding, "When I saw you on the news…I didn't recognize you as my wife. You've changed."

Maybe he was right.

A few days later I returned to work at the university, where news of my confrontation (accompanied by copies of the news footage on mobile phones) seemed to reach mythic levels, and I was suddenly the "American who turned back the soldiers." Although it didn't hurt my ego one bit, it did make me worry—after all, even as the wife and mother of Palestinian residents, I had no legal "right" to stay in the country and I could be arrested or deported without my kids for "trouble making."

It was time to accept the fact that, after eleven months in Safa, and as much as I wasn't yet ready to leave, it was time to start wrapping things up.

Ahmad and I decided on a departure date by the end of the summer, in just over three months' time. I hadn't made any progress in figuring out how to get into the Golden Gate or lay eyes on the underground chambers on the Temple Mount, and although I doubted that I would be able to succeed in this ridiculously difficult goal, I still couldn't shake the idea. For some reason, seeing it *meant* something to me. I just hadn't figured out what.

One thing all the excitement of the previous weeks had given me was perspective. I would have to start asking for what I wanted *as I was*. After all, in the big scheme of things, it didn't really matter if I failed, or somebody said no to me because I was an "outsider," not Muslim enough or Arab enough...real enough, good enough. *To hell with it*, I decided. Next time I was on campus I was going to introduce myself to the faculty at the *Shari'a*, or Islamic Law department, and see if they would be willing to help me on my little quest.

CHAPTER 32

Happy to Help

Many things are lost for want of asking.

- ENGLISH PROVERB

Hebron University's Islamic Law department was on the fourth floor of a concrete building with a railing-less central staircase that reminded me of the one in my house—in other words, a death-trap waiting to happen. I didn't know much about Islamic law, but I couldn't help but think if there was anything in it that addressed little things like liability, they might want to spend a few shekels for a railing.

These were the musings with which I distracted myself as I waited for the dean of the department to finish a meeting with a colleague. Finally the secretary, a kind-looking woman who turned out to be from Safa, let me into the office, where an older man I took to be the dean, and a younger man wearing small, round glasses, sat at a computer, presumably helping his boss with what looked like some technical difficulties.

As I walked in, both men looked up at me, and I took in a breath and set about the business of introducing myself in my usual semi-coherent Arabic.

"*Assalam wa alaikum,*" I said, "I was wondering if you might have a moment..."

As usual, my surprise accent seemed to have the magical power to evoke instant curiosity, and their eyebrows rose in unison. Immediately, the younger man, who introduced himself as Dr. Loai, offered to excuse himself—in English. Sensing that it might be better to keep him (and his English) around, I hastily pointed out that my mission wasn't a personal one.

"Would you mind if we spoke English, then?" I asked, relieved at having the pressure of forming comprehensible Arabic sentences off of my shoulders; especially because I hadn't yet decided what I was going to begin with.

"Why don't you speak Arabic?" the dean asked, using a tone that made me feel as if he was asking, "Why don't you breathe oxygen like the rest of us?"

Embarrassed, I hastened to explain myself and my linguistic sloth (after all, I'd just said I'd been a Muslim for over twenty years), telling him that I'd only lived in the country for a year. Still, he wasn't buying it. So I sat back in my chair and clasped my hands tightly, bracing for the kind of lecture I used to get back home from the older mosque ladies, usually delivered in broken English, about my woeful inadequacy.

I sat, patiently waiting for the harangue to conclude, and by chance glanced over at Dr. Loai in time to catch his expression. It was a look that said *I get it*. It was subtle, but it was there. Suddenly, I had hope again. Maybe this wouldn't be so bad after all.

Clearly frustrated with me and my lack of fluency in the language of our faith, the dean directed Dr. Loai, who turned out to be a practicing attorney as well as a professor, to help me with whatever I needed. So I decided to just spill my guts.

I sat across from Dr. Loai in the small office he shared with another professor, and once I told them the short version of my life story and how I converted and proceeded to explain my obsessive mission in all its misguided glory. Then I waited, expecting some sort of lecture about the volatile nature of the Mount, the difficulties involved, or maybe even a rebuke for the frivolity of my goal. What I got instead, though, was a simple offer of help.

"I'll be happy to introduce you to some people who might be able to advise you," he said. "Why don't we meet next week, and we will see what we can set up."

I happily agreed, and then hurried to a meeting about my first exam with the English Dean, who sprinkled the obviously "important" meeting with offers of cigarettes, comments on my fingernail polish, and a very slimy remark about how I "must have it easier than most women" because I didn't have a husband to take care of. "And, Jennifer, how about going out to grab some lunch?"

Umm…That would be a *no*.

I hung out in the Shari'a department as often as I could during class breaks, and after a couple of weeks, Dr. Loai finally arranged a meeting for me with a retired *Waqf* employee and author/ historian, Muhammad Abu Saleh. He encouraged me to be as clear and open as possible about what I was seeking to do. In other words, just ask.

During our meeting, however, it didn't quite go as well as I'd hoped. In fact, when I mentioned the specific places I wanted to see, Abu Saleh dismissed the topic as altogether impossible, telling me that the Israeli authorities had made the places I was interested in completely off limits. Altogether, I couldn't really tell if he was being sincere or evasive; on one hand he did promise to introduce me at the *Waqf* offices. But when I pressed him on the phone for a possible date, he admitted that he didn't have a *tasreeh*, the permit West Bank Palestinians needed to visit the city, and that it would take a long time to apply for one.

Unfortunately, time was something I had less and less of every day.

So, after thinking it over, I finally decided to just take Dr. Loai's advice and ask Abu Saleh for a contact there on the Mount that I could arrange to meet on my own, as well as the all-important permission to use his name as a reference. Thankfully, he agreed, telling me to present myself at the Trust's offices and to ask to speak to the man in charge.

As Dr. Loai put it, "You are no longer Jennifer Jones, a stranger from America. You are a Hebron Islamic University lecturer, recommended by the university's vice president, the Shari'a Department, and the respected *Waqf* historian, Muhammad Abu Saleh. You have a base here now, you belong."

I didn't know if it would be enough to buoy my case for access to the closed sites on the Temple Mount, but I did know it felt damn good to realize that he was right. I did belong, just as I was.

CHAPTER 33

Temple Mount *Waqf*

Insanity—a perfectly rational adjustment to an insane world.

- R.D. LAING

One of the surprising things about Jerusalem is how awful the traffic is—much worse than anything I'd even seen in L.A. or Seattle, especially once you reached the inefficient roads surrounding the Old City. Unfortunately, the traffic on the day of my meeting with the Sheikh was even worse than normal, because it happened, unbeknownst to me, to be the day of a Papal visit to the Mount. This was not the greatest timing on my part, but I found a place to park my car, and speed-walked through the Old City to get to the appointment on time.

The one good thing about running late was that it made me too frustrated to be nervous. And that was a great thing, especially because I still didn't know what I was going to say to the Sheikh in charge when I saw him. Then there was the fact that I just hated introducing myself to new people, a feeling now magnified by the fact that I had to force myself to do so in this complex and exclusively male domain—all in Arabic.

I made it across from the Damascus gate to the Mount in record time because I used the Via Dolorosa, the least crowded of the Old City streets. Still, although I'd worn what I thought were sensible flats, they turned out to be as slippery as butter on the cobblestones, causing me to trip-and-windmill like a cartoon character with no traction. *Next time*, I vowed, *I'll wear sneakers.*

I managed to make it to one of the smaller entrances only a few minutes late, a deficiency an alert Ethiopian-Israeli policeman immediately sought to remedy. He not only searched my bag and checked my documents, but he decided that I wasn't a Muslim and couldn't go in. Unwilling to waste time arguing with him, however, I decided to leave and get in through another, larger entrance where I could enter without anyone taking notice of me.

The *Waqf* offices were imposing from the get-go. They were located at the one of the entrances to the Mount, and I ascended a narrow stairway into a suite of offices built into an old building on the west side of the area. Taking a deep breath, I expected to be questioned immediately, but realized that the very strict interpretation of Islamic dress I had on made me temporarily invisible—long enough for me to stand in the office's foyer and collect my thoughts.

Finally, I approached one of the guards, identifiable in their blue shirts, walkie-talkies and black pants, and told him in Arabic that I was looking for the offices of the Sheikh in charge of the Islamic Trust. I naively expected to meet his receptionist and perhaps wait for a few minutes until they could see me in. However, the guard was so obviously baffled by my foreign accent and Palestinian appearance that he walked me past the waiting area and straight into the Sheikh's office, where he was in the midst of a huge meeting.

"No...No! " I protested, my stomach dropping as I glimpsed the large gathering inside. "I can wait until he's finished..."

But the Sheikh, seated at a huge, wooden desk in the center of the room, seemed to hear my accent and motioned me in.

"Yes, sister," he called from inside. "Come in."

Reluctantly, I walked into the room where at least twenty men in business suits were seated in a large circle—an arrangement that forced me to stand in the middle as I faced the Sheikh at his desk.

"*Salaam wa alaikum,*" I started, rushing to explain who referred me, followed by a vague, stumbling explanation about being a writer wanting to do a project on Temple Mount architecture and the *Waqf*—which was *kind of* true. It was just the best my Arabic and my addled mind could come up with under the pressure of so many eyes. Still, I half expected a bolt of lightning to come in through the window and cook me for lying by omission in such a holy place.

Then came the gauntlet of questions. They all peppered me with vaguely personal inquiries about my conversion, marital status, and, when they found out where I was living, about my life in Safa and the recent troubles there. It was all very friendly and good natured—not at all like the atmosphere in the English Department, thank God.

I pointed out that I was a teacher at Hebron University. After all, if I had to put up with comments like, "You can call me any time…my wife is used to girls calling me," from Dean Ladies Man, I could use my position to gain some extra cred. It was only fair.

I smiled, they smiled, and the Sheikh ruled that the *Waqf*'s chief archeologist on the site, Dr. Yusuf Natshe, would be "happy" to help me—only I would have to wait until the following week, as he was currently "tied up with the Pope."

I could respect that, and one week later, I was actually early when I arrived for the meeting with Yusuf. After finding the entrance to his offices through a small passageway and up a narrow flight of stairs, I saw that Yusuf hadn't yet arrived. He had an assistant, however, who invited me into his small side office to wait, and as I chatted with the soft-spoken man, I realized that I recognized him from one of the many times I'd been called out as a possible foreigner during my early trips to the Mount.

That day I'd used bad judgment and chosen one of the smaller, northern gates that saw almost no foot traffic. It featured a long, echoing tunnel that led up to the gate's open door, giving the Israeli police, stationed just outside the entrance, clear reception of my kids' loud English as they skipped through the gate's open door and out into the Mount's northeastern courtyard.

Wagif! "Stop," said one of the two policemen, addressing me in Arabic. I assumed from his accent and his dark complexion that he was Druze or Bedouin—either of which could be trouble.

"Where are you from?" he continued, taking my passport and flipping to its photo. "You are not Muslim," he said. "You can't go inside."

"I am a Muslim," I said, "Look at me. I'm speaking to you in Arabic; I'm telling you that I'm a Muslim. What more do you want?"

"You are not a Muslim," he insisted, as if I'd come to this forgotten, obscure portal with a gaggle of Muslim children simply to pull something over on him.

Unwilling to engage in the debate with him, but too proud to call back my kids, who were already playing in the inner courtyard, I insisted that he just call over a *Waqf* guard, the standard operating procedure I'd been through dozens of times, who could then (as Muslims, themselves) question me on some routine matter of faith, confirm my knowledge, and let me in.

For some reason, though, this guy wanted the pleasure of smoking me out as an imposter, or showing off his Arabic. I wasn't sure which.

"No, you say the *Fatiha* to me," he said, referring to what is known as the "Opening Chapter" of the Quran, a portion that every Muslim knows because it is said at the beginning of every one of the five prescribed daily prayers in Islam.

Still, there was something about performing in front this guy—and that's what it felt like—that just pissed me off; he was flexing his muscles as if I were a trained dog doing tricks to satisfy his macho ego. It was my Achilles heel.

His voice rose, and mine did, too.

"Like I *said*, just call over the *Waqf* guy, and he will confirm."

"Just say eet!" By now the officer had switched to English, presumably for the benefit of his partner, a blond, short-haired Ashkenazi, or Israeli of European origin, who, perhaps seeing that the moment offered more entertainment than his cell-phone conversation, hung up and walked over to assess the situation.

"What's the problem?" asked Blondie.

I replied testily, "The problem? The problem is this guy doesn't want to let me go because I haven't kissed his ass enough." I was shouting and pointing my finger at his chest.

Bad idea.

At this, Mr. Arabic flew into a spitting, eye-popping, tomato-faced rage. Luckily for me, however, just then the *Waqf* guard happened over to see what all the commotion was about.

"You! You can't say that to me!" the officer screamed, "This is a holy place! You don't know. I could be a Muslim!"

The truth was he was partly right. I shouldn't have said it; it was a holy place, but there was just something about pushy men that drove my good sense and reason to distant lands. At that bizarre moment, all I wanted to do was yell back, just as loud as he had, and I did, shouting, "Well, then we have a bigger problem than I thought!"

"What?" He turned to his partner, switching languages again to Hebrew, "What did she say?!!"

At this, I turned my back on the officer, dismissing him as so many soldiers had done to me and the kids over the months, knowing full well that I would probably be arrested or at least kicked out of the city for my impertinence. Now, I addressed the silent *Waqf* guard, who obviously couldn't understand the language of the exchange, but could certainly understand the tone (and was perhaps wondering why they hadn't kicked me out already).

"If a Muslim says he's a Muslim, then he's a Muslim, right?" I said, referring to the *Shehada* or declaration of faith that every new Muslim says to convert. "It's a single sentence: 'I testify that there is no God but God, and Muhammad is his prophet.' That's the rule of our religion, right?"

"Well, yes" he answered.

"Then I don't have to say the Fatiha to prove that I'm a Muslim, right?" I said, glaring at the officer, determined not to jump through the hoop he had set for me.

"Yes…that's right."

"Fine, I answered, "*Ashadu La ilah illa Allah, Muhammad rasoolu Al-lah.*" I said, simply, and without a word turned my back on them all, joined my kids in the courtyard and walked away toward the Dome of the Rock, leaving the Bedouin officer to yell after me, in Arabic, "Crazy! She's CRAZY!"

He was only half wrong.

If Yusuf's assistant recognized me as the crazy lady today, he gave no indication of it, but maybe he was too polite to bring it up. Soon, though, Yusuf arrived, poking his head in the office and telling him to follow me to his office next door.

Yusuf Natshe was nothing like I expected him to be. Middle-aged, clean shaven and a little jumpy, as if he maybe suffered from the same kind of coffee habit I did. He looked for all the world like Mel Brooks.

"You were early," he said.

"Yes, I know, I…"

"I don't know why they always send all the foreigners to me…like I don't have enough work."

Uh oh. This might not be good.

"I know why. It's because I'm the one who can speak English around here," he interrupted, not so much talking to me as thinking aloud. Then, as if resigning himself to his fate, he inhaled, laced his fingers together on his stomach, and leaned back. "Well, anyway. Welcome, Jennifer. What can I do for you?"

"Well, I'd like to know about you and what you do here, for one thing."

"Ah, well, that will take some time to explain. But what can I say for now? I am an archaeologist, a writer, a Palestinian. I like to go long-distance bike riding. But I have to deal with so many requests from people who want my time. Just look at this email from someone representing this person—what's his name, yes, Alex Trebek, from a game show. They want to film here for a game? A *game*. Can I allow that? And then, there are always people who say they are someone other than who they really are. You have to be careful and consider the emails and phone calls very carefully. This is a sensitive place."

The guy was no dummy. In fact, I started to realize that his bluntness was probably an essential part of the job, a kind of warning—don't mess with me, I'll find you out. If he didn't even trust Alex Trebek, what was he going to think of me when I finally worked up the nerve to make my request? Rattled, I continue asking random, vapid questions about his work and the work of the *Waqf* in general, which he answered willingly enough. But afraid of an instant and easy "no," I put off being direct for so long I ran out of time. Yusuf suddenly announced that he had to run to another appointment.

Frustrated with myself for wasting the meeting, I left feeling I'd blown it. When I finally contacted Yusuf to ask for another appointment, however, he was out of the country on business, and with no firm indication of when he might be back. With my time in the country dwindling, I decided it was probably best to forget the whole silly idea of getting into the off-limits places on the Mount. Who did I think I was, anyway? It actually felt good to give up.

Finally done with my classes, I focused on taking the kids on a long-deserved tour of the country, where we swam in virtually every body of relatively clean water we could find. We went to the Golan Heights near the Syrian border and swam in the muddy Jordan River, and then hiked to a deserted swimming hole set in perfectly hexagonal shaped volcanic rocks. We returned to the Mediterranean, floated in the Dead Sea, and drove back over to the ancient seaport of Acca, capped with its beautiful green-domed mosque, and surrounded by blue water, crashing against crusader walls.

We even fit in a few more of the kids' favorite places that somehow kept calling them back—Solomon's Pools, Lower Herod's fortress (an ancient bath complex riddled with abandoned cisterns, tunnels, and crumbling mosaics—always deserted, aching for intrepid little explorers to walk its once opulent grounds), and the kids' favorite, the caverns under the Church of the Nativity in Bethlehem.

We were having a great time, but I still had to adjust to thoughts of going home. I was happy that I would be able to see my husband and family, stop being a single parent—and let the kids get to know their dad again. At the same time, though, I knew that the huge loss of daily freedom, as well as the loss of the close family relationships that the kids had developed and clearly now cherished, might make their reentry into their old, rather lonely American existence a difficult one. And then there was the knowledge in the back of my mind that I hadn't been able to pull off all I'd personally set out to do. I hadn't been able to morph my mishmash of an identity into enough of an asset to get into the Mercy Gate or had a chance to get a glimpse of the "Great Sea" that so intrigued me as a subject in Simpson's painting. But I'd done all I could. I'd just have to chalk it up to fate…

I *was* ready to go home—except for all that.

CHAPTER 34

Dog Days

Every problem contains the seeds of its own solution.

-Stanley Arnold

I started closing things down in the house, the power, phone, covering the furniture with plastic, and began our goodbyes to the friends and students I'd met over the year. I even started to feel depressed about leaving my husband's family! After all, I liked them and I suspect they probably liked me, perhaps even more now that our days in the village were dwindling.

One morning, in the midst of our preparations for our coming departure, I finally received an email from Yusuf, saying that he would meet me again. I was surprised and determined not to waste another minute this time beating around the bush. So, I decided to respond to the email referencing exactly what I wanted. After all, with the days quickly dwindling, I didn't have much chance of success anyway (I nervously reassured myself).

Quickly, and before I lost my nerve I wrote out in black and white just why I wanted his help—then I hit send and hoped for the best.

Unfortunately, the next day I received a scathing response from Yusuf, saying that although he would meet me again, it was not the time for "adventurous discoveries," because whatever is found, reported on, or photographed has and continues to be used for nationalistic aims. My desire to go inside the Gate and see the underground structures, he said, could be misconstrued by opposing groups and those small but vocal and powerful segments of Israeli society that were pushing for the restoration of the Temple, *right now*. Then, summing up, he added that he'd never heard of the Great Sea.

Well that pretty much says it all, I thought, sitting at the kitchen table and feeling a little stupid. Actually, I wanted to crawl under the table, as if I'd been slapped on the hand like a silly child. Still, the more I thought about it, the more I realized I didn't agree with his core premise that opening the closed sites must necessarily be dangerous to the status quo on the Mount. It certainly never stopped Israelis from opening disputed sites, complete with artfully placed flood-lighting, placards and pre-recorded storylines to support their exclusive historical narrative of the place—often as a means to excuse confiscation of areas owned and inhabited by Palestinians for hundreds of years.

It was a prominent Israeli Archeologist who first explained the issue to me a few months before when I met him on a tour of the so called "City of David Visitor's Center," located just south of the Old City's walls.

Yoni Mizrahi was well known in Jerusalem as a kind of crusader for the scientific integrity of archaeology in the Holy Land. Formerly of the Israeli Antiquities Department, Yoni joined an organization of concerned Israeli and Palestinian archaeologists to run alternative tours in the City of David because, as he explained, he "objected to the science of archaeology being used for political, or even religious claims." He explained that some politically motivated Israelis—like those at the City of David—misuse digs as a way to "claim territory" instead of truly studying the history of a particular site. This, according to Yoni, is what happened at the visitor's center—run by a notorious right-wing private organization called Elad, which publish guides for its close to 400,000 mostly Israeli visitors touting the place as *the* bedrock of an exclusive Jewish claim to East Jerusalem.

. Unfortunately, the site is also located smack-dab in the middle of the ancient Palestinian village of Silwan, an area Elad and settler groups desperately want for their own.

Problem is, many of Elad's archeological claims are highly controversial. According to Yoni and others, including prominent archaeologist Israel Finklestein of Tel Aviv University, while there are extensive ruins on the site that date back to the ninth century BCE, there isn't a smidgen of evidence that refers to David or his palace. As Yoni explained, "You'd think from all the signs and brochures Elad gives out to the center's visitors, they'd come across an engraving that said, 'Welcome to David's Palace!' But they haven't. They just dig and claim." It was as Raphael Greenberg, another Tel Aviv lecturer pointed out in a 2010 interview for the *Time* magazine article, "Digging up Trouble," "Their attitude seems to be that if you believe in the Bible, you don't need proof...You're supposed to dig for six weeks and then report on what you find. In the City of David, they've been digging nonstop for two years without a satisfactory report." The reason? According to scientists like Yoni and Greenberg, the right wing uses archaeology as a way to "throw out the Palestinians living in the area and turn it into a Jewish place."

Thus, it was this problem that was on Yusuf's mind when I mentioned the closed sites. Not only did he worry that allowing me access to places the Israeli authorities on the Mount deemed "off limits," might spook them into thinking that the Waqf was up to something that might strengthen their claim on the site, but that my poking around and taking pictures might give people and organizations like Elad incentives to interpret whatever I (or more likely, other potential visitors) photographed or described as "evidence" that the site should be theirs. For organizations like Elad, there simply wasn't a concept of accepting history in all of its layers as evidence that the place in essence belongs to all who call it holy. In Jerusalem and elsewhere in the country, history's remains are just another kind of ammunition in the fight for ownership, and people like

Yusuf were justifiably worried that a similar, and exclusionary "City of David" could easily happen on the Temple Mount—and that, my friends, would amount to a new and terrible war that would outstrip any that had come before.

I understood Yusuf's point, but at the same time I felt that the *Waqf* was missing an important opportunity to do exactly the opposite of Elad's agenda; that by opening up and exploring each and every layer of history that they could (without prompting the Israeli government intervention), they could do much to underscore the fact that Pagans, Jews, Christians and Muslims all have long histories on the Mount. I believed, like Yoni, that true history is rich and inclusive instead of exclusive. But I also understood that the *Waqf*, and even Yusuf, himself were representatives of the weaker party, and as such felt as compelled to protect access to each shrinking square inch that they still managed to control, lest they lose access to it all, forever.

Such were my thoughts as I fought to regain my composure after Yusuf's email, but whereas before I—the perpetually clueless convert—might have slunk away like a chastised puppy if someone with Yusuf's knowledge and stature thought I was wrong, this time I decided to say what I thought and see if it made any difference.

I drank a bracing cup of black, Arabic coffee and sent Yusuf an email detailing exactly how I felt—that by bowing to the (albeit, real) pressure to keep places like the Gate and the underground closed to everyone, it would make their position weaker in the end, as if they were disinterested caretakers of arguably one of the greatest archeological sites in the world. I knew it wasn't true, and that each and every *Waqf* employee loved and cared for the Mount, but that wasn't the image they were projecting. I felt that they should make it as open as possible, thereby entering into the modern world of public relations that organizations like Elad were so effective at exploiting...that if they, in contrast, did it the right way, it could actually improve the situation on the Mount.

And as for "discoveries," I doubted that there was anything particularly groundbreaking to discover in either the Mercy Gate, or the underground. After all, Warren and Wilson had wandered around down there looking for proof of the Temple treasure, the Ark or whatever else they could find...in their case to buoy their Christian beliefs, and they even took measurements. I doubted anything I could do on an afternoon visit could cause much of an uproar.

I didn't really expect a response, after all, who the heck was I to say anything?

I decided that we were ready to come home, or as the kids said, to our *other* home. After all, I'd actually surpassed our goal of spending a year in Safa by a few months. It appeared I wouldn't get permission from the *Waqf* to see anything, and I was just plain tired. I called my husband the next day and told him that I booked our tickets.

It was two weeks later that I received a response from Yusuf saying that he would meet me again—why, I wasn't sure—but I wasn't about to miss an opportunity, however slight, that he might change his mind. Imagine my surprise then, as he sat across from me in his small, stone office telling me that he would try to get me the permission I needed. Sitting back in his office chair with a smile, and a faint, bewildered shake of his head he agreed to ask the Mufti of Jerusalem for the access I wanted. Then, he added, "Don't be surprised if the Israeli Police try to stop you." As long as I was prepared for that and the Mufti agreed, however, I would be clear to go.

I was beyond happy on my drive home from the city that day...

so happy, in fact, that I didn't even mind being stopped and playfully interrogated for close to an hour by a tough-looking, tattooed Israeli army unit. One thing I'd unfortunately learned was the difference be-tween honest banter and sexually aggressive mockery. Because this was the former, I could let it go (as if I had a choice anyway), and relax into the soldier's blissful tirade about my using my brains to stay in a nicer place—somewhere like, "*Califoan-ya...*"

Well, he did have a point.

CHAPTER 35

The Haunt of Jackals

Open thy gates of mercy, gracious God!
My soul flies through these wounds to seek out thee.

-WILLIAM SHAKESPEARE

Two days before we were scheduled to leave, I received a final email from Yusuf. I'd all but given up on hearing from him again, and I assumed the Mufti had either declined to give me permission, or he simply forgot about me and my silly request. However, in his usual brisk style, he wrote back a single line—"Between 10:00 and 11:00 tomorrow."

This would be a mere twelve hours before our departure for the Jordanian border. It seemed they'd agreed to unlock the iron doors to the Gate of Mercy and let me in.

The next morning I woke early; excited but very nervous. Ironically, it was the anniversary of the destruction of the First and Second Temples. Known as *Tisha B'Av*—it was a day of mourning across Israel—and, as was usually the case with Israeli holidays, Palestinians from the West Bank weren't allowed to cross into Jerusalem. This, alone could cause a major problem, depending upon the checkpoint (and the mood of the soldier manning it).

Anticipating that I might be turned away, I headed for the city three hours before the scheduled time. Sure enough, a young soldier tried to turn me back at the checkpoint for being "an Arab." But in no mood to waste time driving to the next checkpoint a good twenty minutes away (where the same thing could happen), I put on my friendliest face and explained that I really was an American tourist, as it said on my passport's visa entry. Thankfully, and despite looking very dubious, he finally let me go.

When I arrived in the Old City, it was heavily patrolled by security and police, but eerily absent the normal Palestinian crowds. Instead, gaggles of bubbly tourists roved through the markets clasping ribbon-festooned tambourines and strumming guitars, singing French and Russian renditions of "Kumbaya."

Turning from the main alleyway, I headed into the dark, vaulted Cotton Market. Long and narrow, the place embodied Jerusalem of old—wafts of incense and burning charcoal hung in a perpetual cloud, deepening the gloom, and I felt that I was floating with sheer, unbridled happiness and what could only be described as *relief*.

It was then, as I approached the big staircase that rose out of the market and onto the Mount, that I noticed an elderly ultra-orthodox Jew praying at the foot of the stairs. It was the closest his faith would allow him to approach the place where his Temple was destroyed by the Babylonians in 586 BCE, and again by the Romans in 70 CE, and where Jewish and Muslim blood once flowed together in the streets, spilled by European Christian Crusaders who believed them both heathen.

Stooping, the man placed a lit mourning candle on the step of a tiny shop, which the owner quickly picked up and angrily threatened to throw away. I stopped, transfixed by the scene, as an Israeli soldier stationed at the platform entrance walked over, took the candle and placed it at his feet where no one could touch it. It flickered as I walked by, a perfect symbol of this sad place.

I emerged into the bright sun of the Mount and headed over to the office of the Chief Architect on the Mount, Isam Awwad. There, inside the little, domed building, he told me that Yusuf had instructed him to unlock the Gate of Mercy and the underground cisterns for me, including the Great Sea, even though, according to Awwad, he was virtually the only person the Israeli Police allowed to enter the Golden Gate—even other *Waqf* workers are normally prohibited. In fact, when a professionally dressed young co-worker at an adjoining desk heard where we were going, he begged permission to come along, offering to take pictures for the department. Smiling indulgently, Awwad agreed, the three of us set out from the office, shadowed by an elderly guard carrying a huge ring of keys.

We walked east across the platform toward the Gate, stopping to unlock each of the smaller cisterns on the way. I looked inside, peering down into each one, awed by the clearly visible layers of progressively older stone that made up the surface of the platform, down to what must be the original layer above the chambers, yellowish and worn into smooth, shiny blocks.

We walked on to the Gate of Mercy, but the guard with the keys couldn't seem to unlock the outer gate to the stairs, taking so much time that it gave the Israeli police patrolling the Mount a chance to notice that we were up to something.

Suddenly, two officers were on the scene, taking my passport and questioning me and Awwad, who continued working on the lock as if without a care in the world. Finally, with the help of another *Waqf* guard, they finally got it unlocked and Awwad beckoned me forward, locking the gate quickly behind us to prevent the officers and a growing group of onlookers from following us down the long flight of stairs to its iron-grated doors.

Inside the dark interior, it was much larger than I'd imagined, and as I walked over to the famous archer windows—normally visible only from the outside—where men once defended the city with powerful bows and gazed up at the huge twin domes arching over stained-glass windows, I felt as if there might be hope for me to fit in as me...even here. And as I touched the giant columns topped by carved cornices that some say were gifts from the Queen of Sheba to King Solomon, I thanked God, feeling a wave of peace I hadn't since I prayed at night, alone in my backyard, way back in Oregon.

A cold wind rushed up as two men unlocked and pushed up the large steel lid above the Great Sea. At first, all I could see was blackness and a dense cover of cobwebs, until my eyes focused enough for me to see the immense chamber. Just like Simpson's painting, completed more than 140 years ago, it had remained the same; its immense cavernous space reaching from its dark, black water four or five stories to the ceiling, directly under the paving stones on the Mount. So, too, the same giant boulders jutted up from the surface, and an old pirate-type chest lay perched atop an outcropping of pebbly gravel, like a small island on a river. I couldn't believe that I was seeing it with my own Western Muslim eyes.

AFTERWORD

At Home in Seattle

At home in Seattle, I hear airplanes above me, and see float-
planes instead of fighter jets and drones, green grass instead
of barren rock, and best of all, I can drink real lattes instead of
the abomination that is Nescafé, the unofficial drink of the West Bank.

No doubt about it, life in the Holy Land was hard, sometimes an-
noying and occasionally downright terrifying. It makes me wonder why
I miss it so much.

I was nervous to come back—loving the new me and afraid of a
"relapse" like a junkie fresh out of rehab going back into the real world.
More, the kids are homesick for Safa, hating Seattle for its lack of donkeys, cousins, and mourning the loss of the freedom they had to roam
around and "be kids" in the village. But we keep in near constant contact
with the family over video-cam, and I've promised the kids that we will
try to spend every summer in Safa until we decide where our "permanent" home will be. It's funny, though, now that I'm away from the family
in Safa, I realize how much I miss them. I think I really have a "place"
there now—just in my own way. I even miss the kids climbing into my
house through my windows.

I'm starting to believe that, for us, all roads lead to Jerusalem, and
I still think about moving there for good. After all, in just a little over
a year, the place brought out a sense of independence, confidence, and
even courage in me and my kids that I never thought possible. More,

it taught me that there *are* people who will accept me for the strange hybrid I am—American/Muslim, rather like a brocco-flower, I suppose, odd, but still stronger for the mixing.

Still, the Holy Land isn't some kind of theme park for the faithful; it definitely has its dark side. Yet, as so many who have walked its desert paths, dusty roads, and cobbled walkways know it is *still* a place of miracles. At least it was for me.

I became transformed in the Holy Land, and I found out that finding a place where I "really belong" has more to do with being comfortable in my own skin than finding approval outside, whether it's from my husband, family, or community (although I'd prefer no more calls from the Secret Service). I can even live with hanging around Seattle for a few more years—maybe.

As for my husband, he's got some adjusting to do, poor thing. He's actually uttered the cursed words, "I want my old wife back," and you can be sure I made him pay for that one. You see, it's not that anything obvious has changed, but I am a lot more, well, stubborn than I used to be, and a lot less willing to "take the leg."

But I'm also happier, and I hope the benefit of that will appear in the long run, rather like the beauty of a toned body after a few months of torturous cardio.

And as for my daughter, Amani, the one who started all of this on the mat back in Taekwondo? She came home from school the other day with a poster from a class project. On it, she wrote: "Someone I admire: My mom, because she is kind and she is free."

Now, as I put on my own uniform to attend Taekwondo with her, I pray that she too will always be kind and free of the struggles that I, and a generation before her, have faced.

Author's Note

This memoir consists of memories, observations, and personal experiences that are mine alone. I neither have the authority or expertise to speak for anyone else. In almost all cases I have used real names but have changed a few when I felt the repercussions of my writing may have caused discomfort to the individual. Although I have used actual place names, many of these are controversial, and are in some ways politically, ideologically, or religiously "loaded." In almost all instances I have chosen to use the common English names and spellings with the intention of preserving as much clarity as possible for the reader, and I categorically refuse to intentionally use place names as way to further political or ideological goals. For that, you must look to the "experts." Perhaps the most notable example of this is my use of the term Temple Mount, rather than the Arabic, Haram ash-Sharif or "Noble Sanctuary," and although I find the Arabic meaning more inclusive, I have used the more common Western name without any intentional implication of "ownership." Similarly, I have in most cases referred to city names by their Western spellings instead of their Arabic or Hebrew ones. I hope that any offense I have caused by this choice may be forgiven.

Although it is obvious that I have intense sympathy for the Palestinian cause, I have done my best to present events as they actually occurred without either exaggeration or sugar coating. I do pray for the end of Israeli occupation and settlement, which is in clear violation of International Law, and hope that there will be a just solution to the ongoing Israel/Palestinian conflict for everyone. However, I do not condone any form of government, resistance, aggression, or punishment (collective or individual) that preys on civilians—especially children—and I know that many Palestinians and Israelis feel the same. War is horrible and inherently filled with suffering, yet the abandonment of basic moral standards in war (especially upon an utterly captive population) is, in my opinion, beyond defense. I believe that both sides must hold themselves to standards of International law, including the Geneva Conventions and the Universal Declaration of Human Rights. Absent these basic principles, I fear the Holy Land will remain in a state of perpetual conflict to the detriment of all.

Acknowledgments

I began the process of writing this book almost five years ago, and during the time that I lived, researched, and finally wrote the thing (and, as most writers will tell you, at the end of a book project, the work becomes a vicious thing to be beaten down into submission), I was blessed with the support, help and understanding of many amazingly kind, selfless, and encouraging people—without whom I would never have finished. So, I would first like to thank my agent, Laney Katz Becker, at Lippincott Massie McQuilkin, my editor, Claire Gerus—both amazing beyond belief, Megan Trank, and Michael Short, and Felicia Minerva at Beaufort Books, and especially my publisher, Tracy Ertl at TitleTown. Thank you for taking a chance on this hot potato of a book.

In Palestine I owe special thanks to Dr. Ahmad Atawneh, and Dr. Loai Ghazawi at Hebron University, as well as Dr. Yusuf Natshe, and the entire staff at the Al Aqsa Awqaf, who helped and trusted me out of the kindness of their hearts without asking for a thing in return. I would also like to thank Sa'ed Nashef, Kifah Hamdan, all of my students at Equiom—Maha, Anas, Mohammad, Ayman and Imad—you all kept me semi-sane during some difficult times.

I owe a million thanks to the people of Safa, and my husband's family—too many to mention here, but particularly Khalid, Dr. Mohammad, Huda, Rawan, and of course, my side-kick Manar. You all helped and supported me and the kids while ignoring my many faults—no small thing.

As for my husband, Ahmad, thank you for helping me on this journey, and for your understanding, encouragement (even when you didn't agree with me) and technical help. Thanks to my father and step-mother for forgiving me for taking their grandchildren "over there," and a huge and very special thank you to my kids, Ibrahim, Amani and Karim who were brave and always game for the ride. I'm so very proud of you all.

Finally, I would like to thank the countless people in the Holy Land, Palestinian and Israeli, who show that there truly are good people in the world—even in the harshest of circumstances. I was never in a situation—large or small—in which some stranger wasn't quick to offer assistance. In particular, I'd like to mention Omar Haramy at Sabeel, Yoni Mizrahi at Emek Shaveh, and all of the people who work and hope for a just peace for *everyone*. My heart goes out to you all…and then, last but not least, thanks to my classmates and instructors (especially Jennifer Berg) at True Martial Arts—you all make Taekwondo live up to its reputation of being exponentially better than therapy.

Recommended Reading

BOOKS

Palestine: Peace not Apartheid: Jimmy Carter

This side of Peace: Hanan Ashrawi

I Shall Not Hate: A Gaza Doctor's Journey on the Road to Peace and Human Dignity: Izzeldin Abuelaish

To the End of the Land: David Grossman

Sharon and My Mother-in-Law: Ramallah Diaries: Suad Amiry

Image and Reality of the Israel-Palestine Conflict, New and Revised Edition: Norman G. Finkelstein

Fateful Triangle: The United States, Israel, and the Palestinians: Noam Chomsky

LINKS

Tikun Olam: Make the World a Better Place
http://www.richardsilverstein.com/tikun_olam/

Peace Now (an Israeli peace organization)
www.peacenow.org.il/site/en/peace.asp?pi=51

Women in Black (Israeli and international women's peace group)
www.womeninblack.org

Breaking the Silence, Testimonies of former Israeli soldiers, http://www.breakingthesilence.org.il/

B'Tselem (Israeli peace group) btselem.org

Christian Peacemakers Teams (nonviolent intervention) www.cpt.org

Combatants for Peace (former IDF and Palestinian fighters against the conflict) www.combatantsforpeace.org/event.asp?lng=eng

Sabeel: Ecumenical Liberation Theology Center (Palestinian Christian peace group) http://sabeel.org/

Friends of Sabeel North America, http://www.fosna.org/

Ecumenical Accompaniers for Peace in Palestine & Israel (witnessing and supporting) www.eappi.org

Gush Shalom (Education and direct action by Jewish Israelis) www.gush-shalom.org

Quakers with a Concern for Palestine-Israel, network of Friends groups in North America, www.quakerpi.org

Machsom Watch, (checkpoint monitoring by Jewish Israeli women) www.machsomwatch.org

Rabbis for Human Rights (Justice for Palestinians and Israelis) www.rhr.israel.net

The Parents Circle, Palestinian/Israeli Bereaved Parents for Peace, http://www.theparentscircle.org/

Archaeology in Jerusalem: Digging Up Trouble. Tim McGirk. *Time* magazine (World) www.time.com/time/magazine/article/0,9171,1957350,00.html#ixzz1unq5ZTgH

About the Author

Jennifer Lynn Jones was born and raised in the tiny town of Independence, Oregon, where she converted to Islam from Christianity at the age of fourteen, after reading an English translation of the Quran as part of a high school class assignment.

Jennifer is active in the North American Islamic community and is the author of the book, *Believing as Ourselves* (Amana, 2002), a practical guide for the empowerment of Muslim women. She has written articles for Ma'an News Agency (the largest wire service in the Palestinian Territories) and the *Seattle Times*, and has contributed to The Islamic Society of North America's (ISNA) nationally circulated Magazine, *Islamic Horizons*.

Jennifer lives in the shadow of Microsoft, in Redmond, Washington, with her husband, Ahmad, and their three children.